Broadcasting: Breaking Down the Barriers

Broadcasting: Breaking Down the Barriers

Nick Baker

UNIVERSITY
OF LUTON

press

British Library Cataloguing in Publication Data
A catalogue record for this page is available from the British Library

ISBN: 1 86020 572 0

Published by
University of Luton Press
Faculty of Humanities
University of Luton
75 Castle Street
Luton, Bedfordshire LU1 3AJ
England

Email: ulp@luton.ac.uk
Website: www.ulp.org.uk

Cover Photo: Laguna Design/SciencePhoto Library.
Cover design: Sarah Shrive, University of Luton Press
Printed in Great Britain by Antony Rowe (Reading) Ltd., Berkshire, UK

Contents

Acknowledgements

This is the section I've been looking forward to writing the most. Completing this book has, at times, been challenging and I would never have been able to write it without the help of a whole host of people. It's nice to be able to thank them all now personally. Firstly, I'd like to say a big thank you to all the following who have advised me, kept me in check and put me in contact with those in high places: Tony Cambell for his sporting genius, Jim Ferguson & Joanna Crosse from Meta Media for their wisdom, John Smith, Naomi Boyd, Gareth & Lizzie Allen, Simon Bagge, Lubna Bhatti, Mark Thompson, Guy Panel, Robyn Oneile, Tina Price and George from James Grant. I also want to mention Ed Thompson, Lynn and Steve Smith-Dennis, Andy Leonard, Keith Beard, Kerry Broadbear, Nick Stall, Stuart Garcia, my French connection in St Albans Jasmine Kehal, Dave & Becky Howitt, Lee and Donna Norish, Steve and Sharon Walker, Steve Deakin, Sherrie Eugene, Ozzie Artman, Sammy Mason (don't hold back), Philip Banks, Dennis Batten, Matthew Pick for his poetic verse, Sue Owen, Peter Crooke, Tony Crosse, Malcolm, Steve, John and Ken for their entertainment at ETT Computers in Hammersmith, Janet Haslam, Duncan Jones, Will Haines, Pat, Mark and Tom Pinhorn, Ian & Heather Lings, Jez and Gemma Rowe, Sam Morgan Moore, Nick Baker (No. 2!), John Godel for giving me my first break in radio, Richard Myers for my break into TV and Manuel Alvarado for publishing this book. My friends have also been great. Firstly, my best mate Steve Long who's stuck by me through the highs and the lows, Craig Spafford, Andy Patten, Stuart Crosse, Dominic Higgins, Jane and Adele George, Bob Sherlock, Catherine Hamblett, Christine McDonald, Judy Smart and Briony Baxter. Finally, I want to extend a huge thank you to my family because, no matter what, they have always supported everything I have done. I want them to know I appreciate that very much and also that I intend to pay back every single penny I've ever borrowed from them! My two grans Dorothy Cotton and Doreen Baker, my parents Terry and Janice Baker and my brother Simon who's over in the States!

Nick

1

Introduction

Television is an enjoyable and rewarding profession to work in. You only have to look at the competition to see that it's certainly one of the most popular. Because broadcasting is considered a glamorous career there are thousands vying for only a limited number of places. Those who achieve success have two things in common: dedication and persistence. These qualities appear compulsory if you want to establish yourself in TV.

One or two rejections are usually sufficient to weed out those who aren't serious about a television career. If you are serious, you need to know that although it's tough to break into it's not impossible. All the proof you need is in this book.

Broadcasting: Breaking Down the Barriers focuses on the careers of some of television's most accomplished broadcasters detailing their rise to fame. It also reveals the obstacles they encountered in their journey to the top. It's important to identify these barriers because you will face them too in your own quest to make it in television. There are also interviews with top producers and news editors who give their own insight into the change and development of one of the fastest moving industries in the world.

As a broadcast journalist I have been lucky enough to work alongside some of the people featured in this book. Starting my career in radio, a move into TV was difficult and often appeared impossible. But, as this book shows, my experiences were by no means unique. The people who reach their goals know that rejection is simply part of the process.

This book has two simple aims; to show you what it takes to make it in broadcasting and provide you with the inspiration to make that dream a reality. Whether you're just about to embark on your career or you're already working in television you will find this book engaging, enlightening and indispensable.

National News

2

National News

With the digital revolution already upon us it is sometimes difficult to keep this sudden change in technology in perspective. It may bewilder the viewers as they embark on the process of finding out what it means and whether they want to invest in it. But at least they have a choice over the speed of change. For television professionals and those aspiring to join them there is no such choice, the only option is to climb aboard now or get left behind.

In television newsrooms across the country the new digital technology is having enormous ramifications and changing fundamentally the nature of the jobs performed there. For a start reporters are expected to be skilled technicians as much as they are journalists. It's their job to manage the equipment as well as compile the information. Then there is digital editing. Many reporters are already able to edit news packages on desktop computers. Gone are the days when the reporters' sole task was to write news stories.

The question many people are asking is what will be expected of the national news journalist of the future? The answer can already be seen in part in BBC newsrooms where they are already embarking on the revolution. Most of their journalists are already multi-skilled and represent the new breed of broadcasters. The BBC's 'News Centre' at Wood Lane in London boasts the very latest broadcasting technology of which its journalists form an integral part. Digitally editing pictures, taking live feeds and setting up stories is just part of their job as the Managing Editor of *BBC News 24*, Chris Birkett explains.

> What broadcasting is seeing now is a huge expansion of TV channels due to digitisation. Because there will be so many new channels in the future the only way they will ever be able to run is by employing people who are multi-skilled. This includes journalists. In the current climate, where budgets are getting smaller and channels are getting bigger, multi-skilling is the only way to save costs. It's the future. At *BBC News 24* this has already happened. I have 120 journalists under me and not one of them would have a job unless they were multi-skilled.

With such cutting edge technology already in operation the BBC is providing a fascinating glimpse of the future. Would-be journalists take note! Although Sky and other broadcasters haven't followed suit yet they're likely to when financial constraints start to dictate. As Chris Birkett says, more channels means fewer viewers and with less of those, companies will have to start justifying their costs even more. With this in mind you can forget the TV journalist of old, today's new recruits at the BBC need to be multi-skilled.

> You've got to be computer literate. The personal computer provides the basis for everything a journalist does so you have to know the logistics of a PC. Next, you've got to be the sort of person who embraces technology and makes it your friend. Here at the BBC we're using technology at the cutting edge of the market. Being brand new means the machinery is sometimes prone to failure, so when it goes down you have got to be the sort of person who isn't going to get frustrated and blame it. The '90s reporter has to conform to this. I don't employ people who just want to be reporters and I don't employ people who aren't willing to get into the technology. I employ people who want to be multi-skilled.

So, how do you make it as a reporter at the BBC? The answer is you have to serve your time.

Most national reporters at the BBC start their careers at a local radio station. It's here they learn what journalism is all about. With many newsrooms now 'Bi-Media' they quickly find themselves writing reports for television as well. These days journalists at the BBC are expected to file reports for both mediums, as and when required, even at national level. At London's News Centre all the stories are 'pooled' so material that is filed for one station can also be accessed by others. Reporters will often find themselves writing a report on the same story for both television and radio. The pool of stories at *BBC News 24* is also fed by reports from local stations across the country. This vast network enables every BBC station to access a story quickly and easily.

For reporters at *Sky News* the situation is different. Although the station also provides a rolling 24-hour news service reporters don't yet need to be master technicians. Their main role is to provide up to the minute reports from the field backed up by live 'Two-Ways' (presenter talking to reporter.) The Managing Editor of *Sky News* is Simon Cole.

> We're fortunate here at Sky, although we're influenced by accountants we are not yet governed by them. This means our reporters don't have to double up as technicians. Of course this will inevitably change in the future. As television expands reporters will probably be expected to do more. What will probably happen is journalists will have to learn the basics of something like editing. When you're out in the field this kind of skill would be helpful and cost effective.

Simon Cole has an impressive track record. Working his way up to a reporter then News Editor at ITN before joining Sky, he knows how the industry has changed. More importantly he knows how it's likely to change in the future. If you're a young reporter trying to break into *Sky News* this kind of insider knowledge could prove useful.

> If you want to come and work for Sky it helps if you know what's required from you in the face of change. I would expect you to know the difference between an SNG and a

links vehicle and the difference between VHS tape and Beta SP. You also need to know how satellite works. As much as I hate to say it, although Sky News isn't restricted too much by a financial budget this could soon change. It costs an enormous amount of money to send a crew off to a foreign country so we're already seeing slimmer outfits. In light of this, if a reporter can edit then that's a plus. Skills like that are always useful and the more skills you have the more I would be interested in you.

Of course, when it comes to reporting at national level having a secondary skill isn't the only requirement that helps. Relevant experience is essential. At Sky all main reporters have to be good live. After they have produced a report they are often expected to conduct a live two-way with the presenter. Simon Cole has a definitive answer when you ask him what he looks for in a reporter at Sky.

The thing about news is it's a relentless beast so you have to be prepared for anything. Live stand-ups from the reporters form an integral part of our news output so you must have a bit of spine. Unfortunately, here at Sky we don't have an internal training scheme as such, therefore I have to look for experience. I can't gamble on giving a job to a reporter whose work I don't know so I'll usually look to see whether they have some experience in regional television. The final quality I look for in a reporter is integrity, you've got to be straight. I really believe in the saying you must be nice to people on your way up, after all the next time you meet them could well be on your way down.

Worth noting. Someone else who believes in the honest approach is the Controller of News, Current Affairs and Documentaries at Channel 5, Chris Shaw. As an ITN man himself, Chris knows that to get to the top in this business you have to get on with people. Being a team player is imperative.

As a television reporter you're one link in a large chain, so being affable is important. Here at Channel 5, news gathering can get stressful so staying calm in the face of adversity is an advantage. I also look for people with a lot of stamina. Reporting can be an extremely physical job and very relentless so it helps to have lots of energy.

Reporting at national level is not only relentless, it's also very competitive. This in itself can be tiring. I'm sure many young reporters are dogged by the recurring question: just what is it going to take to break in? Although we all accept it's tough to get your foot through the national door it's not impossible. Channel 5 is just one example of a broadcaster that actively encourages young blood into the newsroom. That's good news if you can fit the requirements.

> I look for journalists with a good sense of curiosity and persistence married with common sense. These journalistic instincts are vital. I also look at people who come to Channel 5 on work experience too. Three of my best reporters first came here on work experience and I really believe there is no substitute for it. I look closely at how someone gets on with others and how enthusiastic they are without being too over the top. If you can show you have a lot of initiative that's how to impress a news editor.

As television news continues its metamorphosis into the digital age it's worth asking yourself one question: are you willing to change with it? The race to bring news onto our TV screens even faster and cheaper is a marathon that will never end. The modern day journalist is a vital part of this race, so stamina is essential if you want to compete. Although the next few years will bring about great change they will also bring with them great opportunities. The more skills you can learn now the more chance you have of exploiting them. National news is a competitive market but it's not impossible to break into. If you follow the advice that's just been given to you from three of the industry's top editors then there's no reason why you can't make it.

Trevor McDonald

Evening News

"Television is a very contagious thing. Once you're exposed that's it, you're infected."

Trevor McDonald is a household name and to millions of viewers across the country he's the number one newscaster. As 'arguably' the most famous presenter in the history of British television, Trevor McDonald is to news what the Beatles are to music, legendary. But when you ask him about his career Trevor remains modest. In his eyes he's just been extremely fortunate.

> I think I've been terribly terribly lucky. I'm honestly quite surprised at just how fortunate some things seem to have worked out for me. When I started doing the news I never dreamed I would get to the position where I am today. When I was younger I just thought I was getting in here to make a living to pay the mortgage. I certainly didn't have any grand ideas about what I wanted to do. If I had my time again I would say a little prayer for the same kind of fortune. I think that may be pushing it though because I've just been so lucky.

Even though Trevor is by far one of the best known newsreaders on our screens he's also one of the most approachable. It's partly this genuine appeal which has made him such a hit with the British public. Just like his character, Trevor's personal history is equally fascinating and first began thousands of miles away in the West Indies. Born and raised in Trinidad, a young Trevor had already started displaying an interest in journalism when he was just knee high.

I'm almost a little embarrassed to say it now but when I was at school I started my own radio station. Although it was only a small outfit we used to broadcast around the school campus on Friday afternoons. A couple of other pupils and myself used to read the news and we'd take all our material off the BBC's World Service. It actually became very popular. At the time I remember one of the teachers came up to me and said, 'Trevor, if it's the last thing I ever do I am going to make sure you get a job in radio.' As it happens he never had to but the thought was nice!

The teacher in question never had to because Trevor managed that side all by himself. After studying for a degree in international politics at college he went on to work for Radio Trinidad as a reporter. Learning the ropes, within a short while he'd progressed to the local television station, Trinidad and Tobago TV. What had stood him in good stead was writing for the college paper and producing articles for various magazines when he was younger.

I think as long as you can display an interest in journalism when you're at university or something then getting a job in the industry shouldn't be difficult, but you need to be determined. You've got to want it and be hungry for it after all any job, no matter what it is, doesn't just slide into your hand by accident. You have got to get after it and chase it and prove yourself. A practical thing that helps a journalist enormously is reading. When you're working in current affairs you have to read voraciously. The idea that you can get on in this business without reading monumentally is a fallacy. You've just got to do it.

Although Trevor's parents wanted their son to go into law or medicine, Trevor always had other ideas. Working as a journalist was a dream he had nurtured from a very young age activated by the most part from listening to the BBC's World Service on radio. Hearing the news correspondents file their reports from around the world was inspirational stuff to a young boy living in the backwaters of the West Indies. It was something he was determined to pursue himself. In later years the dream would become reality after a young man, by now a reporter, had visited London in 1970.

> I had been to London on a trip and while I was there I had gone to see someone from the BBC World Service. I'd told them that if they were ever looking for a reporter then to let me know! At that same time, and what I didn't realise, they had already seen some of my work while they were reporting themselves in Trinidad. No sooner had I got back home I received a call and was offered a job in London. My first job in England was working at BBC'S Bush House and I ended up staying there for three wonderful years.

While Trevor worked for the BBC he received the best possible training in British reporting. Rather than taking his time to adapt to the sudden change in news he threw himself head first into his job. Three years later he joined ITN after writing off speculatively for a job there. The year was 1973. When a letter arrived asking him for an interview it came as a great surprise but nonetheless, when the big day finally arrived, he impressed the news editors so much they offered him a job on the spot. Trevor was so shocked he told them he had to go away and think about it! I think I would do things a little differently now, he admits.

Trevor was the first black reporter on ITN and although conscious of the fact it didn't inhibit him in the slightest. One of the stipulations he had made when first accepting the job was insisting on doing all the jobs every other reporter did. This he duly performed and more.

> I didn't want to report black ethnic minority stories from the Brixton point of view, I wanted to do everything. The big story in my day was Northern Ireland and when I first started I was sent there. It was tremendous experience and a time in my life I will never ever forget. The whole thing was a very big deal for me because I was able to wet my feet, as it were, on a running story of national and international importance. It got me noticed and it also got me the kind of attention which told people I could do this kind of thing.

Before long, Trevor McDonald was an experienced reporter. Not only had he amassed hundreds of general reports he had also been assigned political, diplomatic and sports stories. Many of them had taken him around the world. Looking back, there are many wonderful occasions to reflect on but none more so than one particular time that went down as one of the greatest political events in history.

> I'll never forget the occasion because it was in Soweto the day after Nelson Mandela had been released from prison. It was the first time we had ever been allowed to broadcast from South Africa without requiring special permission from the government. I had sent a colleague to pick up Archbishop Desmond Tutu who I had arranged to interview on top of a flat truck. ITN had hired it especially. In my excitement, what I had forgotten to plan for was Desmond Tutu's huge popularity with the people of Soweto. Wherever he goes the rest of Soweto follows.
>
> When he arrived the first problem we had was actually getting him up onto the truck. There were thousands of people chanting all around and each one of them wanted to be near him. Eventually, after a few attempts, he finally managed to clamber aboard and as ITN cut to us live I started interviewing him.
>
> One of my very first questions was whether he was worried that Nelson Mandela might not prove to be the person to fulfil the dreams expected of him. After a brief pause, a huge smile broke out on his face and the Archbishop replied, 'You know, we shouldn't be thinking about all that now, we should just be pleased that he's free!' With that, he grabbed me by both arms and started dancing me around the truck – all live on British television! I don't think he's ever forgotten it and I certainly haven't as it isn't every day you get to boogie with an Archbishop!

Unlike his favourite football team, Tottenham Hotspur, Trevor McDonald admits he's had his fair share of luck! As one of the leading celebrities in television news he can regularly be seen presenting a whole host of other programmes. Notable examples include *The National TV Awards*, the contentious *Monarchy Debate* and the current affairs show *Tonight, With Trevor McDonald*.

> I think to a certain extent you make your own luck and part of that is being fully prepared for when the break arrives. Of course on top of this you also need the ability, there's no point waiting for a chance if you can't do the job. Being in the right place at the right time is always going to help and the more you put yourself about the more chance you give yourself. In such a competitive industry it's important to keep focused. As long as you know where you want to go and how you're going to get there then you will be alright. Time goes quickly so it's important not to let it lapse.

As a principal figure in news who thousands of young people aspire to it's not always easy giving advice. What works for one person may not always work for another, as Trevor is keen to point out. According to him success in news is down to one thing – hard work.

> I really think there's no substitute for hard work. Nothing comes very easily at all in television and it's only through hard work you're going to get anywhere. You have to put the hours in. When you first start in journalism if you want to get ahead quicker then you've got to learn the craft quicker. The only way you're going to do this is by getting your head down. Often this will mean making several sacrifices but make them you must if you're going to succeed. Journalism can often encroach on your social life and free weekends are never an option. It's all or nothing in this business and if you're not totally committed then you can't expect to get to the top.

It may sound silly, but actually entering the business for all the right reasons is also paramount. With television still viewed by many as 'the glamorous profession' many people are still joining TV news because it looks the part.

I do think you have to have an unadulterated interest in the thing, I'm not too sure you can fake it. There's no point entering any profession if you're not 100 per cent interested in it because if you're not then you won't enjoy it. Along with this interest you have to have a desire to be truthful and honest about what you do.

You also have to be fair and well balanced. It's terribly terribly easy to tell stories from any side or any angle with a particular bias. Telling the unadulterated truth about what's going on should be your only objective and you must never be pulled hither, thither or yon by any kind of personal, social or moral considerations. Journalism is a fascinating way to make a living in society but one must never abuse one's position.

Looking back, Trevor McDonald is right to feel content. The married journalist has been working at ITN now for 25 years and he's still at the pinnacle of his career. Just recently ITN re-affirmed their faith when they offered Trevor a lucrative three-year contract for him to stay. When *News At Ten* moved to its new time there was no question about Trevor moving with it. On top of that the great man of news was also knighted by Prince Charles for his services to British television.

I never expected to work in any place for a great length of time, never mind a quarter of a century! A while back I must admit I seriously wondered whether I should be doing something else because 25 years doing one thing is such a long time. I think the reason I have stayed in news though is obvious and if you're just starting out yourself then you must consider why. There aren't many professions that allow you to span the field like journalism and when I think what I've done it seems amazing. I've covered football in Argentina, cricket in Australia, wars in the Middle East and droughts in Mozambique. If you ever need inspiration to get you through the hard times then just think of those opportunities. News is second to none.

Kirsty Young

Channel 5 News

"Success is when preparation meets opportunity"

Kirsty Young is well known for not only reading the news but making the headlines herself. It seems the Scot is not just flavour of the month but a permanent taste most tabloids just can't get enough of. But despite all the attention she still manages to keep her feet on the ground – thanks mainly to a gruelling work schedule.

> The press attention is a very strange thing, especially when they're prying into your personal life. It happened to me once in Scotland so because of that it's come as less of a shock. The thing with tabloids is they always need people to write about and I'm sure in time they'll move onto somebody else. I'm not really bothered by it because you've got to remember it's only the newspapers, it's a transient thing. Some of the stuff they write, I admit, is incredible and bears no relation to the truth but I don't think it's me they're writing about because they turn you into a kind of cartoon character. At the end of the day they've got a job to do like you or I so there's no use getting your knickers in a twist about what's on page seven of *The Sun*.

Kirsty Young first broke into broadcasting as a runner. Having just returned from a journey abroad she was introduced to a TV sports cameraman who was looking for an assistant. This particular runner was required to do everything from making tea to cleaning the kit and quite frequently Kirsty would find herself up to her armpits in mud. Although the role was just a general dogsbody Kirsty was hooked and she knew right away that a career in television was for her. Waving a chance to go to university she became a freelance runner then worked as an assistant for a small production company. Although she hated the latter, it did give her the experience to apply for a job at the BBC. It was this that launched Kirsty Young's broadcast career.

> The job was a newsreader for BBC Radio Scotland and I must admit I didn't think I stood a chance at getting it. In the end a friend of mine had to physically sit me down and make me fill out the application form. I've got a lot to thank him for. I think more than 700 people applied for the job and when I got it I really couldn't believe it. It just shows that even if you don't think you're qualified enough for something you should always go for it nonetheless. You never know what kind of person a producer or head of news is looking for.

Landing the job also landed Kirsty her first real challenge in a broadcast environment. At just 21 years of age she found herself the youngest person in the newsroom with the least amount of experience. Needless to say the learning curve was steep.

> When I first started it was very intimidating to say the least. I really felt I had to prove my worth. Looking back, if my colleagues were cynical towards me then I don't think I blame them. I think I would have been if I'd been in their shoes. Although it can be uncomfortable to start with you just have to remember that you got the job because the people of importance had faith in you. If they have faith in you then you should have faith in yourself. I personally care for the opinions of people I value but beyond that if someone has a problem with me then it's pretty much their problem. I certainly don't dwell on it.

This wasn't the only test. Next on the agenda was reading a live bulletin. Working at a national station meant there were thousands of listeners and this didn't exactly make the prospect any less daunting.

Before I did my first bulletin I remember running into the toilet and gagging I was so nervous. You put pressure on yourself just by thinking about everyone who's listening. People tell you to block that thought out but you never can. To make matters worse I was introduced by a guy called Mike Russell, who is Scotland's equivalent to John Humphreys. The mere fact he was mentioning my name was enough to make me shake in my shoes and when I spoke it was as if someone was playing tricks with my voicebox. I guess it must have been a good few months before I started to actually enjoy reading the news. It's important to enjoy this element of broadcasting because if you don't then you can easily come a cropper. When you're nervous more mistakes can happen and then it's easy to make a fool of yourself. Throughout the years I've seen hundreds of presenters who clearly don't enjoy live broadcast and it amazes me why they put themselves through it.

After working in radio for a couple of year's television beckoned and Kirsty was soon presenting the lunch-time and evening news on local TV. Many broadcasters use regional television as a training ground for higher things and so it was with Kirsty whose aspirations lay with national news. Regional TV is not only used by many as a stepping stone, it's also a good place to make all your blunders as Kirsty herself discovered on a couple of occasions.

There were two notably embarrassing moments for me. The first was not long after I had started in TV when I completely name checked the wrong programme. I was presenting *Reporting Scotland* but for some reason at the very end of the news I said, 'And that's all from *Scotland Today*' which was on the other channel! I didn't realise my mistake until the producer started yelling down my ear piece. The second instance was when I got a terrible fit of the giggles. I was reading a news story when suddenly I just erupted with laughter – tears were literally running down my face. I don't know what triggered it but the fact I knew I would probably be getting in a lot of trouble with the producer just made me laugh even louder. As soon as we came off air nothing seemed funny anymore so it just shows what adrenaline can do. Luckily I didn't get the sack!

After presenting in Scotland Kirsty made a move across the border (several in fact) when the BBC asked her to work on their *Holiday* programme. For some inexplicable reason she didn't need much persuading and was soon jetting off around the world. But, as she's keen to point out, the job is much harder than it looks.

> It may sound glamorous but I can assure you it's not. For a start you're permanently living out of a suitcase. Although the places you visit are incredibly beautiful you only get to see them for a couple of days before you're back on the plane again headed for somewhere different. I worked out once that on a two week period I had been on 15 different flights. Now I don't care what anyone says that's not glamorous. When you're working on a programme like *Holiday* you can wave goodbye to any normality as you have no life, people forget that. Although it's nice in the beginning the novelty soon wears off just like anything else.

One thing that has never worn off with Kirsty is the excitement of live television and it was this she missed while working abroad. It came as no surprise to many, therefore, when she accepted her current position as the presenter of *Channel 5 News*, a job she adores. The programme is well respected in the industry for its unique approach to news and no-nonsense interviews. With Kirsty at the helm the viewing figures have rocketed. What's even better is Kirsty has managed to prove that even in a predominantly male environment getting to the top is never impossible.

> I think if you're a woman working in television then you're a bit more of an easy target. Newsrooms can sometimes be notoriously macho places and I'm still convinced some men think women have a certain view of the job that's different from their own, whatever that is! Although the macho thing does go on, I don't think it will stop anyone who's determined from making it. I'm sure loads of people say

things about me that I never hear about but because I don't hear them they don't affect me. You can't afford to let things like that get to you anyway because you've got enough to focus on without needless worry.

With her career most definitely on the up, it seems for now at least there are very few obstacles left for Kirsty to clear. With this in mind, who better to offer a little advice for those of us just about to encounter our first?

I think people should be open minded about what they want to do. Just because you try one job in television doesn't mean you should stick at just that if you fancy trying something else. There are so many interesting jobs in TV from floor managers to producers. When I first started as a runner at one point I thought I wanted to be a camera operator but because I was open-minded I decided to try journalism. This decision really worked out for me because I eventually found that presenting was my favourite job. The other thing is don't run before you can walk. When you do get your first break you can't expect to be a producer in six months or a presenter in a year as it usually doesn't happen that way. I still read some newspapers articles that talk about my 'overnight success'. It makes me laugh because I have been in the business 12 years now and I've worked hard to get to where I am. If you're just starting out then you'll have to serve your time too. Be patient.

Although patience is most definitely a virtue there's still nothing wrong with a few tips to speed along progress. If you're planning to follow in Kirsty's footsteps here's what you should be doing.

If you want to excel at presenting, or even reporting, then watch the people you admire most and think about what it is that makes them good. Is it their composure or honesty? Next, see if you can apply those things to yourself without taking away your own personality. You don't need to turn yourself into an identical presenter but just season your own performance with that you've learned from watching the professionals. These days all sorts of people work on television so if you've got a unique individuality that works on screen then apply it. The good thing about TV today is there's not an accepted view of beauty. You can look at 25 very different faces and there is no one look. That's great.

Although this may be true for the most part one look that's being tipped to stay is Kirsty Young's. As the battle between the television networks continues over who woos her, it seems this particular presenter will be in vogue for many years yet. Although many people still assume Kirsty has risen from the ashes overnight the important thing is you know better. If you're planning a career in presenting yourself, then it's worth bearing this in mind.

As this book went to press Kirsty announced she was planning to leave Channel 5 News after signing a new contract with ITN.

Jon Snow

Channel 4 News

"There's no such thing as a neutral journalist and there's no such thing as a neutral human being. But there is such a thing as a fair journalist and that is what we must all aspire to."

Precise and to the point is what a good reporter ought to be and this is exactly what Jon Snow is like when you talk to him. He's been in the business too long for the wool to be pulled over his eyes and as a journalist he knows exactly what the score is.

> If you are not made angry by the things you discover then you're going to be a lousy journalist. In this business you've got to be fired up, shocked, horrified, upset and seduced by real life events. If a story doesn't stoke up your emotions then you're not going to move the viewer. In television news that's exactly what you should be doing.

Jon Snow has an admirable quality. He's a prime example of someone who doesn't just say something he goes out and does it. These days they are a rare breed. How many people do you know who can talk a great game of tennis but when they finally get to hold a racket they can't even hit a ball?

> Life is short so you must know what you want to do then you must go out and do it. If you're interested in going to Afghanistan to try to get the Taliban then pitch your career towards foreign affairs. If you're interested in local

government then go for politics. The cardinal sin is to get sucked into something you're not interested in – if you're not interested in it then you'll never be any good. News is an amazing opportunity to tell people what's happening. If that genuinely doesn't turn you on then people will know and they'll turn you off.

The history of Jon Snow and journalism first starts at Liverpool University. While studying for a degree in law John worked part-time for BBC Radio Merseyside on a late night student show. After finishing college Jon went on to work as a director at a youth centre and ended up staying there for three years before deciding to go for journalism. When he did finally enter broadcasting he'd only made up his mind to become a reporter six months earlier. This quick action is again evidence of someone who really does act on his instincts. Some would argue this defines a good journalist.

It wasn't an amazingly conscious decision to become a reporter, one day I just liked the look of it. But it wasn't easy to get in. When I first started applying for jobs in the media I must have been turned down at least 30 times in the first couple of months. One thing that went against me was I wasn't prepared to travel outside London. If you're just about to start applying my advice is don't limit yourself like I did. In this business you've got to be totally flexible about where you're prepared to work and what you're prepared to do. If you're flexible like this then you won't have a problem easing open a few doors.

It was at LBC radio station where Jon got his first break. Although it wasn't based there at the time, LBC is now at Grays Inn Road, a key media hub of London. The site is home to ITN and also houses ITN's *Channel 4 News* and *Channel 5 News*. Jon began at LBC the very first day it went on air and held the elevated position of 'phone operator'. LBC was one of the first ever stations to try live phone-in debates and a young Jon Snow's former counselling skills were required to deal with the 'plethora of psychotics' who subsequently rang in. A short time after, most of the reporters at the station were sacked during a dispute and Jon quickly found himself promoted to newsreader. This was just one of many lucky breaks Jon Snow was to be blessed with.

> I must admit I do attract luck. I remember the first News Editor I ever worked for at ITN once told me, 'Jon Snow, you may not be very bright but you are extremely lucky' and it was true. When I first started as a TV reporter things just happened in front of my camera. One time I got sent out to cover President Jimmy Carter's visit to London for the early evening news. I was preparing to do a live stand-up for the last minute of the programme. The very second the camera switched to me I noticed the president walk just behind me accompanied by his usual entourage. I knew it was an opportunity I couldn't miss so I turned around and shouted, 'Hey, Mr President! How would you like to go out live on British television?' A startled Jimmy Carter replied, 'Sure, why not?' and was soon standing right beside me. It was such an exclusive the network decided to cut into the next programme to give me extra time.

Although it may have been lucky timing that the president was walking behind him, it's important to note here that Jon grabbed the opportunity with both hands. As reporters ourselves I'm sure just seeing the president walk nearby would have been exciting enough never mind shouting at him. Imagine the nerve it takes to turn away from a camera which has just switched to you live. Could you do it? The courage and initiative required are obviously a formula well worth remembering.

> Although I class myself as incredibly fortunate I have to say I've made my own luck as well. In the beginning of my career I worked ludicrously long hours which meant I was practically living in the newsroom. This meant the chances of a story breaking around me was obviously a lot higher.

The golfing genius Gary Player can back this up with his famous adage, 'The harder you practice the luckier you get'. Away from the golf course reporters could do worse than ignore this advice. The more time you spend in the newsroom the more chance you have of hitting a hole in one. In journalism terms this means landing the big story.

Jon Snow may not be a golfer but as a journalist he's certainly a class player. Working hard at his game meant he broke into television news relatively quickly. Jon joined ITN in 1976 and within the space of a few years he was working as their Washington correspondent in the United States. Then in 1989 he replaced the Channel 4 News presenter Peter Sissons after Sissons was poached by the BBC. There the present broadcast history of Jon Snow ends because after a move to ITN's *Channel 4 News* he's stayed there ever since.

> I think I work on the best news programme in the country. It's very pro-active which means I get to interact a lot with the people I interview. Not many other programmes allow that kind of engagement.

There's no doubt that Jon Snow is *Channel 4 News*. For the past nine years he's helped mould it into one of the most progressive news programmes on British television. His quick wit and determination to get the truth from people, especially politicians, has earned him a fearsome reputation. But isn't this the kind of thing all journalists should aspire to whether they're just starting out or not?

> Never be afraid to ask questions, after all that is what journalism's all about. So what if you're just a fledgling reporter? Your search for the truth must be your main goal and you'll only get to the truth by asking questions. It's simple. Of course not every journalist abides by this and they are the idle ones in the industry. Unfortunately, there are a lot of them about.

Although Jon Snow is always on the quest for knowledge, he's more than happy to tell you what he's learned. As a young journalist this can prove very enlightening.

> You must be focused on what you really want to do. When people tell me they want to be the reporter Charles Wheeler or the presenter Kirsty Young I ask them why? What is it

about these people you like? Often they can't say so I answer the question for them. Charles Wheeler is an exceptional reporter because he totally immerses himself in every story as if it were his last. Kirsty Young is a talented presenter because she's so natural in front of the camera, so relaxed and so balanced. My advice is discover where your instincts lie then focus on them. If you can do that you'll go far.

If there is anyone in television worth aspiring to it's Jon Snow himself. He's often regarded as one of only a handful of people in news whose unique personality cuts through the confines of something that is sometimes regarded as a dogmatic medium.

Broadcasting is an extraordinary business employing extraordinary people. You've got to ask yourself whether you're extraordinary enough to fit in. Are you inquisitive and hungry to know more? Do you wake up in the morning and want to know what's happening in the world? If these symptoms sound familiar then you're extraordinary too because you refuse to accept things without asking questions. One problem journalists face these days is that the modern media is too interested in how a story sounds or how it looks. They are too pre-occupied with the packaging. For good journalists it's still the content that counts.

That's not the only problem with the modern day media. In this day and age where supply far outweighs demand on an ever-increasing scale, salaries can be shockingly low. With lump sums so small it's often hard to swallow.

I know the low pay thing is a real pain in the beginning of your career but there's nothing you can do about it. For every person who turns down a job for this reason there are always a thousand others who will jump at it. In the beginning you've just got to sweat it out, if you're any good then you'll eventually be paid a great deal. Suffering is what weeds the winners out. People who are good will make a lot of money.

Another problem is experience, or should I say lack of it. In the beginning if you don't have any it's hard to find work. Of course the problem then is how do you find work if you don't have any experience? According to Jon there's only one way to break this paradox, persistence.

You've just got to keep going and going and someone will eventually give you a break. They always do. When I first started job hunting I knew absolutely nothing. I had no contacts and I didn't know anyone in the profession. But like I said before be persistent, be flexible and you'll be fine. Belief is a wonderful thing.

There's no doubt that belief is a powerful tool in anyone's mind and if put to good use can drive through anything. As is often said, 'believe and you will succeed'. But even when you've managed to break into television news and you're finally working as a journalist the belief must continue. TV is by far the most powerful medium in the world and you must believe that what your doing will have an effect on the viewer. Stimulating reports educate and education can change almost anything. If that's not power in your hands then what is?

Katie Derham

ITN

"Be nice to people!"

If you're looking to someone for inspiration in national news then you need look further than Katie Derham. During her quest to become a top newsreader and reporter, the 29-year-old has faced every kind of challenge. Starting from the bottom, with no contacts or knowledge of the media whatsoever, Katie has shown that if you're prepared to work at your career and make sacrifices then a formula for success is not impossible.

> I know what it's like when you're trying to break into broadcasting and the first thing I'd say is don't get too down-hearted. If you don't get the first thing you apply for try not to dwell on it. Everyone I know who's tried to get into journalism via the tea room or a post-graduate course has always had rejection after rejection after rejection. It seems to be standard. The hard thing really is just getting your foot in the door. If you meet someone at a party who knows somebody else who works in a television newsroom then my advice would be to abuse that contact shamelessly! Unfortunately, television is not a business in which you can afford be too shy.

Katie Derham grew up in Cheshire and although she harboured slight aspirations towards journalism during her teenage years it was actually economics she chose to study at university. After graduating from Magdalene College, Cambridge in 1991 it was time to make an important decision in her life, the first of many to come.

When I graduated it was reasonably poor on the job front. With an economics degree everyone told me the only place I could go and work was in the city, either that or do a law conversion course. My heart wasn't really in either. I finally ended up getting a job at a chamber of commerce which was both boring and unchallenging. I was nominally helping out at trade fairs but I think being in charge of the stationery would have been closer to the mark! It paid my rent in London but that was about it. Then I was made redundant and I was unemployed for quite a while. It was at this point that I decided I might as well start applying for jobs in media. This was, after all, what I was interested in.

Katie had just encountered her first major crossroads but rather than sticking to the same route she opted for a change in direction. Choosing journalism meant she was picking a route she knew nothing about but she still went for it nonetheless. With no one to really guide her it was a case of finding out about the media herself. Using her period of unemployment as constructively as possible she set about getting as much work experience as she could. Her first port of call was BBC North.

I worked on a programme called *File on Four* and also the Radio 5 drive time show. It was absolutely fantastic. Everyone was a really good laugh, most people wore jeans and they were able to have a good time. Obviously they worked hard when they had to but they knew how to relax too. I was converted almost immediately. The thing that struck me about broadcasting was there were lots of different things to do each day and it was a really nice environment to work in. Within the first few weeks I was taught how to edit and use a tape machine and it wasn't long before they let me go out and vox-pop. (interview everyday people on the streets.) It was great. It's nerve racking when you first get invited to spent a couple of days at a station but you've just got to get over that.

Working for nothing in a strange environment is a major test of character. If you've got a degree from Cambridge as well then the temptation to take a paid job in some other line of work must be strong. If the urge was for Katie then she wasn't showing it. Remaining resolute she instead rose to the challenge and vowed to learn as much as she could.

> Every person I met on work experience was really confident and successful and there was me with no idea what I was doing. I think the only thing you can do in this position is to get stuck in, offer to help out as much as possible and ask loads of questions. It's the only way you're going to learn. If people think you are genuinely interested and interesting then they'll give you stuff to do. As soon as you've done something practical no one can take that away from you. When you then meet the next person you're able to tell them that you've got some experience. In the beginning it's a knock-on kind of thing.

It wasn't long before a knock-on led to Katie's first break. After spotting an advert in the BBC's internal magazine *Ariel* for an administrative position she applied and got it. Her first paid job in the media was at Broadcasting House working as a secretary at Radio 5. Although it wasn't a newsroom position it was a foot on the ladder. The only direction she could head now was up.

> When I got the job at the BBC it gave me a real buzz just walking into Broadcasting House. I couldn't believe I'd got a job there and it took a while to sink in. Naturally, you have to serve your time as a secretary but a number of things happened shortly after which really worked out for me.

The manager Katie was working for suddenly had his contract changed which meant Katie didn't have a role as such anymore. She was offered another secretarial job but in the meantime was sent on attachment to a radio business programme. Although she wasn't offered a full-time job on the show she was told that if she went freelance then she would be offered as much work as was possible. It was a gamble that paid off.

> I thought it was possibly a completely random thing to do, to go freelance when you're not qualified or really that

experienced to do it. Luckily, I started as a researcher on junior production shifts working on the business programme *Money Box*. Radio 5 was launched shortly after and three more business programmes were commissioned. As a result our department suddenly expanded and needed more people. Because I was already there I was offered a broadcast journalist contract.

If ever there were a classic case of 'right place right time' this was it. But aside from that, it's important to note that it was only what Katie deserved. It was her decision to try broadcast journalism in the first place that led to her initial break at the BBC. After that a brave decision to go freelance paid off too but only because she was willing to take the risk. A career in broadcast journalism is full of opportunities but one of the hardest things is sometimes to know what route to take. At the end of the day lucky breaks are there for the taking but they're usually proceeded by lots of hard work.

Katie Derham's first break in TV came in 1996 after she received a phone call from the producers of *Film '96*. It transpired they needed a replacement for one of their reporters, a certain Kirsty Young, who had just been offered the Channel 5 job. Katie had been highly recommended. After a short meeting she was offered the post and the job involved filing location reports for the popular film programme. What Katie found amusing was it was something she had watched regularly since the age of eight.

Not long after, television work on the BBC's *Working Lunch* and *Business Breakfast* followed and after that an opportunity to work on the current affairs programme *Here and Now*. As the latter was based in Manchester it meant commuting regularly from London. Then, towards the end of 1997, Katie got a call from ITN to find out if she was interested in going in for a chat.

ITN was looking for a media and arts correspondent and I was interviewed for that position. I think what helped is I'd worked in a newsroom before but the producers didn't know that before they met me. When they realised I'd got that kind of experience naturally it counted in my favour. I was very pleased when I got offered the job because for me it was much more my scene to be working on a daily news programme rather than in long term current affairs. I started at ITN proper in January 1998.

Reflecting on her career it seems remarkable that Katie Derham has come such a long way in such a short time. Even though she was never afforded the luxury of a solid background in journalism she has still managed to rise to the top. If you analyse her career closely it's testament mostly to her willingness to take risks and doubtless hard work.

I sometimes think they're going to find me out! Honestly, I feel incredibly lucky to be doing my job but at the same time it's not as if I haven't put in the hours. Believe me there have been plenty of those. What's helped is the right place right time scenario and also making sure I've waved and smiled cheerfully in the middle of frame offering to do the night shifts. Things have certainly happened a lot sooner than I'd ever imagined, but then if you work hard that's what can happen in television. You're given the opportunities.

Advice is never the easiest thing to give but Katie has the following if you want to make an impression in television news. In the beginning it's a question of persevering even if it seems you're getting nowhere.

When you're trying to break into broadcasting always try to keep positive and cheerful. It's tough sometimes I know but you must keep going. Sometimes you will think, 'Crikey, how many more hundreds of letters do I have to write before I get a decent break' but keep persisting and it will happen. In a way I think you've got to be quite innovative. Think of different ways of meeting people and ask others if they know someone in the business who they can introduce you to.

Be prepared to be completely multi-skilled and be nice to people. People are usually only too willing to help out but only if you're pleasant. When I first started I got lots of help from nice technicians, friendly mentor managers and other colleagues who would happily spend 30 minutes sitting down and talking me through scripts, voice training and that kind of thing. This kind of advice is worth its weight in gold but if you're stroppy, arrogant or too shy then you won't get any of it. Be cheerful and upbeat as people remember that.

One thing many people remember about Katie Derham is that fateful news bulletin one day in 1998. You may remember seeing it or reading about it yourself in one of the tabloids. It was only her second week of presenting on ITN when an innocent slip of the tongue resulted in a storm of publicity. Right at the end of a Sunday bulletin instead of saying, 'The next news will be at five to six' Katie read, 'The next news will be at five to sex!' Whatever was she thinking?! As you can imagine, she's never quite lived it down.

I still can't believe how much publicity that got! When I came out of the studio I admit I got a ribbing from the guys in the office but that's all I thought I'd get. I figured some of my friends would ring up and tease me as well but not the papers. When the press office told me that *The Star* and *The Sun* had phoned up I nearly died! It just shows that when you're under the spotlight you can never afford to get too complacent!

Even though she's anchoring one of the most prestigious national news programmes on British television Katie Derham isn't taking anything for granted. What got her there in the first place was complete focus and commitment and this is something she plans to continue. According to Katie a successful career is all about being positive, if you can harness that power then there's nothing to stop you achieving your goals. The other important thing to remember is never give up. As Katie herself can testify, you'll rarely get a taste of success without first sampling a double dose of rejection.

Although it's sometimes been tempting I've never thought of giving up. I'd be lying if I said I didn't have periods where

I've been miserable, when all my friends had jobs and I didn't, but it always gets better. Rejections come but if you keep going they'll always be followed by a break. You've got to keep the faith. For me just working in broadcasting gives me a fantastic buzz and it's definitely worth all the effort.

Local News

3

Local News

If you're an aspiring television journalist with high expectations in the national arena there's one particular domain you're going to have to do battle in first – local news. Although it's not national territory it's equally competitive and requires just as much commitment and persistence to break into. Very few of today's on-air personalities will have made it to the national forum without first working locally themselves. As a place where you learn, practice then perfect your art, it's also the place to make all your mistakes.

With so many media courses being run today the competition for jobs is extreme. At the minute 25,000 students are all studying the subject. Compare that figure to the number of actual jobs in the industry and you've got yourself awesome competition. But don't let that depress you. If you possess the right kind of qualities and go about things the right kind of way then stepping into local news should be no problem.

One person who can confirm this is the editor of Sky News, Michael Wilson. He knows a great deal about local news. Before taking up his current position Michael worked at Carlton TV in Plymouth and was the youngest regional editor in the country. At just 26 years of age he also made the headlines by being named in *Broadcast* magazine as one of tomorrows' top 10 high-flyers.

> I think local news is the most important area in television. Without experience in this or other local fields like

newspaper or radio it's unlikely you'll progress to national level. In TV you have to practice your art whether you're a presenter or reporter. You've got to be able to write to pictures, have an on screen presence and obviously, if you're a presenter, you need to have the skills that make you authoritative as well as accessible. Local news gives you the chance to develop all these. You can experiment to a certain degree and if you mess up no one's going to come down on you like a ton of bricks. It's a chance to hone your art and practice what you feel is your own style.

I don't recommend mimicking other people you see on television because it's important to develop your own persona, your own personality and your own style of writing. It's alright to look at the people you feel are good, work out what it is you like about them and then adapt it to your own style – but not to copy them. I know a lot of controllers at radio stations who get fed up with listening to demo tapes which sound just like Howard Hughes. What they're really looking for is the next Howard Hughes and the same applies to news editors in television.

Now we've established just how important local news is the next question is how do you break in? Firstly, with such stiff competition about it's vital to present the best possible curriculum vitae. As you no doubt already know the only real way through the door is by showing that you're serious about a career in the media. When you meet a news editor they're going to want proof that this is something you've always wanted. If you've only recently decided that you'd like to try television because it looks fun, it's fair to say you don't stand a chance. Your résumé will reflect this.

Although I'm now a journalist I first started answering phones for a talk show in local radio. Not only was it in my spare time, I did it for nothing. When I get a CV across my desk I look at it very closely. The person might have a first class honours degree or they might have a diploma with distinction but I won't be interested in them unless they have made some effort to get practical experience in local media. It's important to do something like hospital radio or reading a traffic and travel bulletin because it shows you have an interest and a desire to get on. You can't expect that just because you're brilliant academically that you're going to walk straight into a job in the media. It doesn't happen that way unless you've got very, very good contacts. In a CV I'm looking for someone who has made the effort and someone who's prepared to learn the skills. Most local TV stations don't have training schemes so they want someone who at least has some nous about them. If you can't get free work at a local radio or TV station then how can I expect you to get an important interview?

Even if you've managed to get the kind of experience someone like John Humphrey's would envy, there's still no guarantee of a job in television. Standing in line alongside thousands of other people with exactly the same kind of background is unavoidable. How long you stand there though is your choice and if you're the type of person who doesn't like queuing then your only option is to jump into action.

The first thing you have to do is target as many regional stations as possible. When you're looking for your first break you can't expect your own local station to offer you a job. Apply everywhere and anywhere, it's the only way. Next, arrange to meet as many news editors or heads of news as possible face to face. Meeting them in person is important because only once they can put a name to your face are you likely to start getting anywhere. Speculative letters accompanied by CVs alone rarely pack a punch. Once you have met your contact be sure to ring them every month thereafter just to remind them you're still around. This may sound pedantic but it shows you're keen. You'd be surprised how many people don't follow up meetings with calls and are soon forgotten.

Finally, if you think the days of offering your services for free are over just because you've been working in radio, I recommend a re-think. There is no time for modesty if you want to move into television. Offering to help out at a station at weekends not only shows willing it also gets your face noticed. The other thing to consider before you make the move into local news is how much the industry is changing. As broadcasting is altering, so too is the role of the journalist. Just as in national news budgets are getting tighter and it's often the journalist who feels the pinch. Not only are salaries low, many reporters are expected to do much more for their money. Many stations already employ video journalists who film their own news stories and other stations expect reporters to edit their own material.

HTV in Bristol is a good example of a TV station that is fully armed with the latest digital technology. It was the first in Europe to fully adopt 'Editstar' – an American system that allows a reporter to edit packages on desktop computers. Rather than using conventional Beta tapes, stories are shot on much smaller digital DVC tapes. Once filming is completed it's left to the reporter to write, voice and edit the report before it goes on air.

The reporter records his voice through a lip microphone which is linked to the computer in front of him. Editing is then carried out by use of a conventional mouse. Despite sounding complicated many reporters like Editstar and more stations are now considering adopting it. The Head of News at HTV, Steve Egginton, says there are many benefits to employing such a system.

> HTV was one of the first places in the world to embrace digital technology and as a result that involved a huge change in the newsroom culture. It means I'm now looking for people who haven't just got journalistic skills but technical ones as well. Reporters here must be able to use the system and adapt to a digital environment. It has been a sudden change in the way we operate but the benefits for the company are great. When we bought Editstar we saved 14 technical jobs and were therefore able to increase the number of journalists. We also employ three video journalists now. By saving money on the technical side, we've been able to invest more money into journalism and as a result I believe we've improved the product.

A number of stations in Europe and America now use the very same system but there are still reporters in this country who have never heard of anything like it before in their lives. Some even refuse to believe it! If you're one of those people then it's probably wise to learn as much as you can about digital editing now. The way things are headed it may not be too long before most places are forced to commit to it. Cue Steve Egginton.

> The craft of journalism is changing fast. When I first started it was just you, your pen and your notepad. It's more complicated now because there are more elements to consider. I think the good thing about the digital system we employ at HTV is that it gives the journalist the chance to work alone from beginning to end. Because they script, voice and edit their own news packages, reporters have total control over their reports and that's a good thing. It means they're not reliant on other people.

Change is something that's all too familiar with the former Head of Programmes at the capital's regional station, *London Tonight*. Simon Bucks says our only option is to brace ourselves for more change yet.

> After working in television in the 1970s I think the days when television was *the* industry to get into because it was such fun may be over. Although there are still a lot of enjoyable elements to the profession, companies have had to bolt down the financial hatches a lot more. They're still businesses after all. Journalists naturally form an integral part of cost cutting and we can expect more practical skills from them in the future. The times when a reporter went out with a large technical crew are well over. You just don't need such a big outfit any more. Bearing all this change in mind, if you are considering entering the profession you have to think about where it is going in the future and whether you're prepared to follow with it. The bottom line is there's going to be an awful lot more required from reporters. If you don't like that thought then perhaps you should seriously consider a different career.

Despite a sea change, broadcasting is still as popular as ever. Many news editors say they receive on average more than 50 speculative job applications a week and that doesn't include applications for work experience. The waiting list alone for work experience placements at some stations is eight months long. This outlines the level of competition in broadcasting just at regional level. To make sure you're top of any news editors list you've got to start recognising what changes are taking place now and how they will affect the newsrooms of tomorrow. If you can reflect on a CV, or in an interview, that you know the direction television is heading then you're one step ahead of the crowd. In a market where competition is extreme this could mean you're one step closer to a job.

Richard Bath

Carlton

"Luck doesn't happen, you have to create it. You have to give people the opportunity to provide you with a lucky break."

Richard Bath is a good example of someone who has made his own luck. He's also a prime example of someone who has experienced reporting and presenting at the highest level. The excitement and immediacy of TV journalism has been in his blood for decades and is a subject he is more than qualified to talk about.

> When I look back on my career there were occasions when I would say to myself, 'Is this all worth it? Do I really want these people to treat me this way? Is this really what I want to do with my life?' I think there are a lot of people who have actually left journalism and I can understand that. But at the end of the day, what kept me going is the fact I love working in newsrooms. News gives you a tremendous buzz that very few jobs can match. I think reporting is very much like flogging a used car, persuading people to do something that's invariably against their better interest. If you want to be a reporter you have to be a bit of a salesman.

When you speak to Richard about journalism you get the feeling he not only harbours a great love for the profession but also a resentful kind of respect. I say resentful because there have been times in the past when Richard has been close to calling it a day.

> If you're just about to enter the business I recommend you think long and hard about whether you are strong enough.

Just when you think you are on the crest of a wave a huge breaker can crash down on you from nowhere and sometimes it can be hard to keep your head above water. That's news. It helps if you're the sort of person with a thick hide because when you first start out you just don't know when someone's going to kick it. Broadcasting is that kind of business.

After studying Communication Studies at Birmingham's Aston University, Richard started his career in 1975 at the city's main radio station, BRMB. Knowing the basics of radio, which he had learned at college and on work experience, was serving him well. Using the station as a training ground to learn his craft Richard flew to Canada to visit relatives and ended up working for *The Columbian newspaper* in Vancouver. It seemed he had managed to enter the media business with relative ease.

Getting your big toe in the door can sometimes be the difficult part but I think everyone knows the best way in is through work experience. That's what I did while I was at college. When you're young you have got to show an interest in the subject by working weekends in your own time, making cups of tea – that sort of stuff. It's tried and tested. Although you may not like the idea of working for nothing you had better get used to it. These days it's the only way anyone manages to get their first break.

In Vancouver Richard worked as a sub and reporter but a year later he'd jetted back to London to start a job at a news agency. The nationally renowned IRN (Independent Radio News) in London was next on the list. IRN provides news to more than 200 radio stations in Britain.

The good thing about the media is you can move around and no-one asks any questions, it's the nature of the business. When you are young, especially, this can be character building and you get the chance to work in a lot of different environments. If you're the sort of person who likes stability though, forget it. In the beginning of your career stability is virtually unheard of, particularly if you're working as a freelance. It's a very competitive market and it's no place for the squeamish.

It was Radio 4 that attracted Richard's attention after IRN as well as a stint in Hong Kong where his first daughter was born. Next on the agenda was his first taste of presenting as well as his first major crisis.

> I got a job at *BBC London Plus* as a reporter. The programme was fronted by John Stapleton and when he went on holiday I was offered the chance of filling in. At first I was all nerves and life was fairly strained to say the least, I mean you are really thrown in at the deep end. However, I managed to survive the initial shock and after a while I began to relax and enjoy it. It was about this time I decided I'd like to make presenting a full-time job. I remember thinking, 'This is it, I'm really motoring now. It's all the way to the top from here on.' How wrong I was! The next thing I knew I was looking for a new job.

Just when Richard thought all his perseverance was about to pay dividends, the programme format was radically changed. Richard discovered that whenever the producers changed the set, the opening sequence and the theme music they invariably changed the presenter too. His contract wasn't renewed and Richard quickly learned just how disposable a presenter can be.

> I was totally knocked for six. It was the first real time I had experienced anything like it and I don't mind saying that to begin with it was hard to cope. For the first few days I just shut myself away and tried to make sense of what had happened, but of course you soon realise that isn't going to get you anywhere. So, rather than moaning about my predicament, I became hyperactive and hit the computer churning out hundreds of applications. I also phoned up as many contacts and news editors as I could. Looking back it was as if I was connected to the mains supply because I didn't stop until I had found another job. In a situation like this, phone bashing is the only option. If you don't start

acting then the only direction you're headed is backwards into an abyss.

Around this time what Richard found also helped was talking to someone else in the industry who understood what he was going through. In his case it was the well-respected journalist Martin Bashir who later shot to fame for his candid interview with the late Princess Diana.

> After you have been totally let down by someone it's important to talk it through with a friend. It just so happens that Martin was my shoulder to cry on. I remember sitting on a bench in Wandsworth Common with a bottle of beer on one side and Martin on the other. I talked with him for hours asking him, 'Why me? Why now?' – you know the usual questions. I've got to say that throughout my career Martin has been crucial in keeping my head straight when all else seems to be falling apart. It's vital to have a genuine friend to listen to your ranting. It's simply unfair to rely solely on your family.

Richard's constant phone bashing eventually paid off and soon he was presenting ITN news bulletins overnight, in the mornings and at weekends. The job gave him several years of relative security. But then ITN moved to its current premises at Gray's Inn Road at precisely the moment a huge recession hit broadcasting. Last in first out meant Richard was suddenly out of work yet again. Automatically the survival instinct kicked in and he had soon found work at Anglia Television in Norwich and then the BBC's World Service Television Channel. Once the dust had settled at ITN it was back to Gray's Inn Road.

> When I returned to ITN it was seven nights a week, 24 hours a day, real nervous breakdown stuff. In the end it was a case of 'these people aren't going to get me down, I'm going to survive'. At the time I was actually making a lot of money but my quality of life was basically non-existent. When you've got a family to consider you've got ask yourself whether it's actually worth it. After living that kind of life

for a while there comes a point when you have got to choose between two things, money or a life? For me it was the latter and when I was offered the job at Carlton TV in Plymouth (formerly Westcountry TV) I jumped at it. With the studios based in Devon obviously it's a totally different experience and I must admit I do miss London sometimes. But on the plus side I have a good standard of living down here and it's nice to have your niche. Carlton lets me loose on other projects too so life's not so bad.

During his career Richard also fronted the popular *This Morning* show when the regular presenters Richard Madeley and Judy Finnegan were away. On top of that an array of corporate jobs and shifts for BBC World Service kept him busy.

When you first start in the business to say the learning curve is steep is an understatement. Try vertical! But that's good because it makes you a better, stronger person. Before you enter broadcasting you have this view that because it looks easy then it is easy. This vision is soon shattered. Personally, I would say that after working in news for so long I definitely don't take anything for granted, when you're working live you can't afford to. But on the plus side television is a medium which is very rewarding and that in itself is one of the great things about it. You certainly can't get bored easily. No one day is ever the same and you always have to be ready for the unexpected. That's exciting.

Most people who enter the media are rarely forewarned about the nature of the business. To say a typical career is a rollercoaster of a ride is an understatement. Just when you think you have finally seen the last drop you're suddenly confronted by another one which tests your resolve yet again. Richard Bath has his own way of dealing with times of stress.

Everything boils down to self-confidence. You cannot afford to lose it. I have always had this vision in my mind of a little box in which I keep my self-confidence. It's like a sort of strong box in your head. I actually imagine turning the key and locking it in there and whatever is going on around me it's there intact, untouchable. When the crisis, or whatever it is, has passed then I mentally unlock the box, I get my self-confidence back out and it's there unscathed. The good thing about this is that whatever someone may have got at they haven't dented my self-confidence. At the end of the day this is vital because your self-belief is your survivability. Lose that and you're in big trouble.

As he readily admits himself Richard Bath has experienced every kind of high and low TV broadcasting has to offer. That's not bad considering how many there are! But at the end of the day the question is, does he believe all the heartache is really worth it? Are there better ways to earn a living?

I daresay there are less stressful ways to pay the bills but I can't think of anything I would rather do. Television newsrooms are populated by some of the best and not a few of the worst people you're likely to come across. The trick is to keep the worst at a safe distance and enjoy the company of the best. I've always felt fortunate to have the support of family and friends through the hard times. Plenty of people I have worked with along the way have fallen prey to the stress and insecurity of the business. I've seen marriages and families fall apart and some people go on to lose themselves in a bottle. The price of working in the media can be very high. But don't let me put you off, as those are only the worst stories. Television is fantastic and very addictive, it's certainly a drug I don't think I'll ever be able to kick. When things are going well it's by far the best profession in the world. Why do you think everyone wants to get into it!?

Claire Montgomery

Tyne Tees

"Be determined, have faith in yourself and you'll get what you want."

If you want to know the level of focus and determination required to break into local television then Claire Montgomery is the person to speak to. Since the age of 15 the Tyne Tees reporter has committed her life to making that dream a reality. One consideration that's spurred her on is the extreme competition. Noticing thousands of other people were also after the same job prompted her to work even harder.

> It's far more competitive now I think than a few years back. When I was at university the personnel officer from Meridian Television gave us a talk about local TV and put the whole thing in perspective. He told us there were 11,000 students studying media nationally and out of that number only a thousand would get jobs. Pointing at my class he said out of us 90 per cent wouldn't even make the grade. He finished the talk by stating we could either accept what he had just told us or be one of the few people who instead said, 'You're wrong and I'm going to prove it.

Claire proved to be in that minority and after graduating managed to break into regional television within 12 months. What helped her along the way was never taking anything for granted and entering the profession for totally the right reasons.

> I'm pretty fortunate because during my career certain people have always given me sound advice. One person was a producer at Radio York. He told me that if I wanted to get

into the industry then I'd get in but if I was going into it because I wanted to be a celebrity then I'd be out of the back door faster than I came through the front.' I've never forgotten that.

Claire realised she wanted to work in TV when she was 13. Watching Philip Schofield on the children's programme *Going Live!* proved inspirational and gave her a goal she was determined to attain. When she hit her teens she secured her own show on a local hospital radio station and after that spent four weeks working on *Harrogate Festival Radio*. Although it wasn't Radio 1 it was essential experience in the bag.

> The younger you can start getting experience the better. I think it's more difficult now because the kind of people who are looking for work experience tend to be much older than before. These days people answering phones at radio stations are graduates because there are a lot more degree courses in media studies. That's not to say it's impossible to get work experience when you're younger of course – only you're going to have to be more persistent. That's not such a bad thing because persistence is something you're going to have to get used to anyway.

For Claire, working on the festival radio proved very useful and provided her with a springboard into BBC local radio. Writing off to local stations and offering her services for free later led to work at Radio York. The odd weekend quickly developed into weekday shifts and she was soon promoted from tea maker to junior journalist. After passing her driving test Claire found herself behind the wheel of the radio car and it was at this point she was allowed to start interviewing people for daytime programmes. All this aged just 18. Moving down south with her parents to Gloucestershire it wasn't long before she was producing reports herself.

> The stories were light fluffy pieces about leisure centres and fêtes but they led onto harder stories. I remember being paid 10 pounds a day. The radio experience was great and I don't think you can work in local telly without it. Although both

mediums are quite different one definitely leads on from the other. As soon as I'd amassed enough relevant experience to warrant applying for jobs in television I sent out loads of letters. One of those was to Tyne Tees.

Tyne Tees Television is based in Newcastle and after a successful interview Claire started life there as a sub-editor. In television a sub-editor or 'sub' is usually the first position many new converts to television find themselves working in. The role varies from producing the early morning GMTV 'opt-out' local bulletins to working the late shift. This means writing the next morning's stories, often until late at night. As you can imagine the hours aren't sociable and many journalists find at this stage the commitment just isn't worth the hassle. Those who stick with it however are usually rewarded with reporting shifts within a couple of years and it's then they choose whether they want to produce, present or report.

> Commitment is a big must in broadcasting and almost everybody who enters the profession finds theirs is tested at some stage. I don't know one person I work with who hasn't had to endure unsociable hours for a period in their life. The time I worked at a radio station during university is a good example. I was up at four thirty in the morning to start work for five then working until one o'clock in the afternoon. After that it was back home to bed for a few hours then up again at five o'clock to work on my dissertation. After finally going to bed around eight o'clock I was back up again at four thirty.

Serious commitment! Of course just because you work anti-social hours in radio doesn't mean you escape the same if you then decide to work in television. Working as reporter means you are on call 24 hours day seven days a week. This isn't always everybody's idea of an ideal job.

> Being a television reporter is not a nine to five profession. If you want to work in TV news you've got to really want to do it. Good journalists are all the same in that they want to be the first people to report the news. You have got to care

about what you are telling your audience and when something happens, even if it's in the middle of the night, you've got to want to be there in the thick of the action.

One other important element to consider about television is how different it is from radio. While some people consider many parallels between the two in reality they are worlds apart.

Everyone thinks television is just radio to pictures but the truth is far from it. You don't need as much dialogue in TV or to signpost things as much because the pictures do the talking. When I first arrived from radio I didn't realise this and the challenge for me was to have to use a completely new dimension to illustrate a report. Pictures speak for themselves whereas in radio the challenge is to create pictures through words.

It's also perhaps pertinent at this point to compare radio presenting with presenting on TV. When a presenter is confronted with a camera things are not as straight forward as some professionals make them look.

When you're presenting on the radio you've always got the option of closing your microphone if something goes horribly wrong or skipping something at a second's notice without the listener knowing. You're not really afforded the same luxury in television. Firstly, you've got people talking to you through your ear piece so your concentration levels have to be high, then you have to look as if you're genuinely interested in what you're talking about. Expressions need to look sincere. As a presenter you're also part of a team and if you let yourself down you're also letting down the people behind the scenes. You're one link in a very large chain. As a radio presenter you're in charge of your own destiny and pretty much left to your own devices from dropping stories to counting out your own bulletins.

As a high-flier in the world of local news it's worth asking Claire for a few tips before she disappears into the land of the Nationals. If you're currently standing where she was just a few years ago, contemplating whether you have a future in broadcasting, it's comforting to hear from someone who's already been there.

> Before you do anything consider how competitive broadcasting is and decide how genuine your interest is in news. This is important because it's the love of your job that's going to drive you forward and keep you going. If the interest is there then try not to worry about whether you'll get the break – it will come. At the end of the day somebody has got to do the job so why shouldn't that person be you? Don't come into television because you think the money is good, when you first start it isn't. Increased competition is driving wages down but the queue to get into broadcasting is getting even longer.

> Finally, you've got to be determined, as like with any profession, and I recommend you start gaining experience as soon as you can. Even if its writing articles for a local magazine at college my advice is do it. Before stations will even take you on for work experience, editors are going to want proof that you're interested in news at a basic level. When you finally get in somewhere for work experience make yourself indispensable. It doesn't matter whether you're running errands or working as a receptionist – the important thing is it leads onto greater things. I started as a receptionist at a radio station once and I eventually ended up as a reporter.

Inspiration is one thing, another is making sacrifices right from the start. If you're willing to work for little or no money at inconvenient times then you're already ahead of the game. How many people do you know in other professions who would be willing to work weekends and bank holidays for nothing in reward for a small salary at the end of it? Not many I'll warrant.

The job of making it into local news is tough but not impossible. Whether you make it is down to what you're prepared to trade for the privilege. If the answer includes your social life then a future in broadcasting is not unfeasible. As far as Claire herself is concerned she's already got both eyes fixed firmly on the future.

At the moment I feel I've still got a lot to take in and Tyne Tees is a great place to work and learn. Down the line, network television is something I could probably go for but I think you've got to consider how different it is to local TV. You've got to get a good grounding in local telly first because you can make mistakes here and experiment. In national telly there's no room for error because at the top editors don't expect any. In regional television news you don't have to work through the night, that's a bonus, whereas network involves night shifts. You also face longer hours. When it comes down to it you've got to decide between quality of life and a career. As reporters we dedicate a lot of our life to a career in local television whereas if you work in national news you've got to dedicate all your life to it. That's a big difference.

Nick Owen

Midlands Today

"Be determined, have faith in yourself and you'll get what you want."

For a man once described by a magazine as an 'unknown, unsexy, uncharismatic, anonymous sports reporter from the Midlands,' Nick Owen has come far. Unlike many presenters who have fallen prey to the turbulent waters of the television industry, Nick has managed to stay afloat. But during his career there have been many occasions when he has almost been submerged himself.

> Television is a wonderful profession to work in when you are on top. Apart from being a professional sports person I think it's probably the best career going. But one thing I have learned is that you must never get complacent. If you do that's when you suddenly get bitten. Looking back, there are times when I think maybe I should have been a bit stronger, a bit more thick-skinned but then nothing can compare you for the low points.

Nick Owen has an established career in both news and sport but is best remembered for his partnership with Anne Diamond on the daytime show, *Good Morning with Anne and Nick*. At its peak the programme pulled in a massive 15 million viewers a week. The show ran consecutively for four years in the early 1990s and Nick admits that particular time of his life was one of the best. When the decision came to take it off the air Nick was totally devastated.

> I was absolutely stunned. There were always rumours about it finishing but that doesn't really compensate for when the

event actually happens. When the controller, Alan Yentob, decided to axe it I was really hurt because I had put so much into the show, I mean so much live TV a day requires an enormous amount of energy, preparation and emotional strength. People think you just turn up five minutes before the programme goes out and then leave as soon as the end credits roll. Unfortunately, it doesn't quite work like that. When you're interviewing several different people a day then you've got to read up on them. The day after the show had finished what was embarrassing was sitting in the departure lounge at Gatwick Airport. All the papers were carrying the story on their front page. Everyone was reading about it and it was extremely uncomfortable.

This was a testing time in Nick Owen's career, but one he admits has made him stronger. Although at the time it seemed like the end of the world, he knew there was only one direction he could follow.

You have just got to get over it and look forward. At the time I had a wife, four children at private school and a big mortgage so things like that tend to stimulate action. There is no option but to keep going and you find certain things help. With me it was friends I could talk to and other people in the business who understood my predicament. You'll find that most of your colleagues will know exactly what you're going through because they'll have experienced it in some form themselves. Also, I find that although I can be very sensitive and easily hurt I do have an inner strength that eventually evolves into a sort of anger. The anger isn't directed at anyone in particular – it's just something that fuels me. In the beginning you go through a period where you just think you must be absolutely useless at the job and no good to anyone but you have just got to snap out of it.

Nick's first foray into television began after a career in newspaper and radio, a traditional route for many journalists. As a boy of nine, a young Nick Owen always knew he wanted to be a reporter.

Starting his career as a trainee journalist at the *Doncaster Evening Post*, writing obituaries and golden wedding anniversaries, he later moved to the bigger *Birmingham Post*. Eventually he joined BBC Radio Birmingham at Pebble Mill.

> I moved onto radio because I got very disillusioned with newspaper reporting. It is so easy to stamp your own interpretation on a story. Also, I didn't like the way news editors kept telling me what point they wanted to get across, even if it wasn't strictly accurate. I have never been into the sort of journalism that twists the truth. With radio and television, at least, the main protagonists can state their own views and to me that's much fairer. As a television reporter you are much more the devil's advocate and that's what reporting is all about.

These days, especially, it's refreshing to meet a reporter with such a genuine stance. But Nick says to get ahead in this business you have got to show your true colours.

> You have to be true to yourself because if you're not people will find you out. For a start, you must never stitch people up because integrity is important in broadcasting. I have always made sure that I never talk behind people's backs because you can't afford to get a reputation for criticising others. I don't think I would have got this far if it wasn't for the people I have met along the way who asked me to work again. If I had treated then badly then they wouldn't have asked me so it's never ever worth it.

During his early days Nick had to compete with what is now regarded as standard competition in the broadcast industry. The first job he applied for in radio attracted 700 applicants alone. Rather than being defeatist in the light of rejection Nick just kept applying until finally getting that job at Pebble Mill. One thing that helped is that Nick had worked in local newspapers. Many news editors at radio stations consider this kind of journalism provides the best possible training.

Since Nick was always interested in sport, when he finally got the chance he decided to move into it permanently. Starting off by reading the odd sports bulletin he worked his way up to sports editor on local radio. Presenting a five-hour sport show on Saturday afternoons soon sharpened his live presenting skills. After mastering radio and learning all about broadcasting, his next move was to ATV (later Central TV). Reporting and presenting both news and sport It was also time for him to learn what the nature of the business was really like.

> In my early days there was one occasion when someone who was important in the scheme of things at a particular TV station appeared to be concerned about my arrival and apparent ascendancy. One day he advised me that presenting and reporting were not areas where my strengths lay and that I should stick with commentating. He said I had a good voice and that was where my future lay. Presenting and interviewing are things I have always prided myself on and when I mentioned what this person had told me to a few other people they said it was pretty obvious why he had said it. Those kinds of things don't happen often but when they do it is important not to let them dent your confidence. When you're at the beginning of a career comments like this can knock you.

Professional jealousy is not the only thing to be on guard for as you start to climb the television career ladder. Snipers armed with poisoned pens can also try to shoot you down. This happened to Nick when he landed a job at TVam in 1983 – the launch of breakfast television in Britain.

> It's the usual scenario, when you're up there you are an easy target. If I think back about some of the stuff that has been written about me in the press it seems unbelievable. I mean, some of the reports are so vitriolic and gratuitous. Sometimes it seems a few journalists are just intent on making your life hell just for the fun of it. At the end of the day presenters are only doing the same job as newspaper reporters, that is essentially giving information. I think half

74

of them are just jealous because they're not in the same position as you. The thing about television is that if you make it look easy people always assume anyone can do it. People in the press nearly always dismiss TV as an easy option, they have no idea. I remember one report in *The Sunday Times* once described me as the person who earned a genius's salary for an idiot's job! If only they had known how much money I was really on. Probably considerably less than that particular writer!

Throughout the years Nick has worked on a variety of programmes outside the newsroom. Travelling the world for the holiday programme *Wish You Were Here* Nick presented two game shows *Hitman* and *Sporting Triangles*. He also commentated on the 1988 Olympics and 1990 Italia World Cup. Although he has a lot more goals he would like to convert before he finally hangs his boots up looking back on his career he has this to say to budding journalists.

The first rule in this business is you've got to be patient. When you first start out don't try to run before you can walk. If you do and you're not prepared you will regret it. I remember when I was working on the Anne and Nick show young researchers would constantly be complaining about their lack of progress. Most of them were just 21 years old. You have got to earn your opportunities. OK, so there are always going to be the people who make it early on – so what? Those people are rare and most of us have to serve our time.

The other thing is always be enthusiastic and show an interest without overdoing it because that can put people off but at the same time be prepared to get your hands dirty early on. It's a question of getting the right balance. Finally, give everything 100 per cent, I always do. Whether it's reading a one off local news bulletin, interviewing a local councillor, or hosting the Olympic Games I spend an enormous amount of time preparing for it. Never underestimate preparation because it's essential, especially at the beginning of you're career when you are trying to impress.

Today Nick Owen's main job is presenting *BBC Midlands Today* in Birmingham. The programme goes out from the very same studio Nick read his first sports bulletin from 20 years ago. If he had his time all over again, what would he change about himself?

> I think the one thing that has held me back more than anything in my career is a lack of self-confidence. In one sense it has been an advantage in that I seem more accessible, you know the boy next door type, but people have always said I should be more assertive and pushy. That's always easier said than done. If I had been more assertive then I think I would have been more thick-skinned and not hit so hard by the setbacks that inevitably occurred. No matter how good you are setbacks always occur and it's important to deal with them properly.

Climbing the career ladder in television can be an arduous task. Just when you think you've got to grips with one rung you discover the next one is missing; the result? Not only does your ego take a bruising you've also got to summon the strength to begin the ascent once again. It begs the question how do people ever reach the top?

> I think you are always looking for the day when you can sit back on the patio in the setting sun with your gin and tonic and say, 'Ah, I've finally cracked it!' I believe the secret to success is not really ever being satisfied with yourself and instead striving for better. I know I still am.

Although it may be a few years yet before Nick finally gets to taste the gin you can't help thinking he will. When you speak with him you sense he'll never give up until he finally feels he's made it. It's this sense of drive we all must possess if we're going to make anything of our own careers and if you're just about to break into broadcasting then make sure you start as you mean to go on. Only by striving for the best can we compete with the best and in this business, like Nick says, that's what we must all be aiming for.

Joyce Ohajah

Carlton

"The day you think you have learned everything is the day you stop achieving. Learning is a life long commitment."

If you think getting to the top in broadcasting is all about the right kind of schooling and meeting the right kind of people then think again. Although it may help the chosen few, for the majority success in television comes down to two things – ambition and persistence. Joyce Ohajah can confirm this as she's needed plenty to get her own career on track. Raised in Walthamstow, East London, an area with high crime and few jobs, Joyce is proof that if you're committed enough then anything is possible. Joyce served most of her broadcast apprenticeship in the United States after moving there when she was 19. As far back as she can remember she says she's always had something to prove.

> I think growing up in a poor area definitely gave me more grit. As a youngster I used to look around me and dream of the day I moved on. Going to America was important because it allowed me to experience different cultures and attitudes. It's a big world. The thing that attracted me to the United States is the Americans have a great perspective on life and they really believe you can do anything if you put your mind to it. I like that attitude. If I'd stayed in this country I don't think I personally would have developed as much confidence to succeed.

To sow the seeds of success, belief is a vital component. Joyce discovered this in America. By continually nurturing her confidence she soon discovered that anything really is possible.

When I first went to study in the States I remember attending a speech class. During one lesson the teacher asked all the students what they hoped to do when they graduated. When she came to me I told her I wanted to be a newspaper journalist. As I'd always enjoyed writing I thought it was a safe and respectable profession to break into. Then she moved onto the girl next to me and asked her the same question. The girl replied she wanted to be a television presenter. On hearing this I couldn't help but laugh – I figured it was the kind of job you could only dream about. But a while later, it suddenly dawned on me that at the time I had totally missed the point and I was the stupid one for not dreaming enough. I have learned that if you don't dream great things you will never achieve them.

One thing that's spurred Joyce on throughout her career is the love of the job. If you like something enough then there's no limit to where you can go. At the moment Joyce is a freelance news reporter for ITN. She is also a senior reporter and presenter for Carlton TV's regional news programme based in Nottingham. Her work for Carlton recently won her a BT Journalist of The Year award (highly commended.) On top of that Joyce has also turned her hand to showbiz reporting including interviews with Gary Barlow and the Bee Gees.

My parents always taught me to go for anything I wanted and this has definitely stood me in good stead. If you enjoy something and want it badly enough then there's no stopping you. These days I think it's important to be a good role model to youngsters and let them know that you don't have to go to the top schools to reach your potential – look at me, I went to an inner city London comprehensive. I always wanted to be a journalist, that much I was sure of, and I never let anyone talk me out of it. When teachers told me I was aiming too high it made me even more determined to succeed.

Joyce first entered the industry after finishing a degree in America. Her first job in a newsroom involved cutting articles out of the newspapers, making phone calls for other people and making coffee. Although it wasn't rocket science, it was a foot in the door. She used her time to learn as much about other jobs in the newsroom and watched closely how the reporters, presenters and producers did their jobs. She also volunteered to write scripts and do as much as possible to prepare her for the job she really wanted – Reporter/ Presenter. One day, when the newsreader called in sick, Joyce got her chance. It shows how important preparation can be and, of course, it helps to be in the right place at the right time.

In the television industry some people say you're never really part of the business unless you've lost your job. Of course knowing that doesn't make it any less painful when the deed actually occurs, as Joyce herself discovered. She learned this while she was working in Rockford, Illinois when a cruel twist of fate meant her losing not one but two jobs in a row.

> Before you enter broadcasting, I recommend you look at the facts. One of those is that no job is ever 100 per cent secure. When I got laid off the first time I was devastated because I had just moved all my gear to Illinois lock, stock and barrel. I was told I had to go because I was the last person to join the company. It's common policy in the States. Unfortunately, I wasn't prepared for it and I took it really badly. I remember being low for a couple of days but then eventually pulling myself together and dragging myself down to the job centre. As I had been on television a lot at the time, I could tell quite a few people recognised me – it was quite embarrassing. When I got to the front desk the woman there asked me what kind of job I was experienced in and what I was looking for. When I told her I was after TV work she raised her eyebrows and said, 'I can tell you right now dear you won't find jobs like that in here!'

Joyce's philosophy has always been that everything happens for a reason and being made redundant was no exception. Although she had never been unemployed before, it brought to life all the unemployment stories she herself had covered as a journalist.

I think the whole experience meant I could relate to people much better after the event. As it happens I was only out of work for two months and four weeks of that were spent on holiday in England. I don't class that stage of my life as negative because I learned a lot about myself and besides, it wasn't long after I had returned to the States that I landed another job. The position was created especially for me at a station in North Carolina and I worked there for over two years before the company again changed hands. Just as before, last in meant first out but this time I had managed to fix a job within an hour of leaving.

Joyce was head hunted by a regional radio station and ended up presenting the drive time news for a station on the East Coast. As well as hitting the radio airwaves, she also put together a TV proposal for a half-hour current affairs show and was commissioned to produce 12 programmes for a new regional TV channel.

Like I say, everything happens for a reason and when you enter broadcasting anything can happen. Although I lost a couple of jobs it led to better things and in fact spurred me on even more. The media is such an amazing industry and working for a music based radio station was one of the best jobs I've ever had. Sometimes it was hard getting up in the mornings when I was presenting the breakfast news, but every job has its down sides. It was frightening sometimes when people said mine was the first voice they heard when they woke up in the mornings! The good thing about the news is you're often the first person to tell someone something. As a journalist this feeling can be a really rewarding.

In television news the opportunities are vast. If you don't like one job then there are plenty of others to choose from. Researching, setting up stories and forward planning are equally important and you may even consider working on the news desk and working your way up to news editor.

Everyone has strengths so you've just got to find out what yours are and use them to get you where you want to go. You may find that you're an excellent live performer or you're better suited behind the camera as a producer. In the beginning it's important to be flexible and find out what you're good at and then take things from there. There's no hard and fast rule that says just because you trained as one thing then you must stick at that. Many reporters become producers and it's often these people who are the talented writers.

Joyce knows that working in television is, without doubt, one of the best professions you can choose. But because it's good it's also very popular and this in turn creates a problem – extreme competition. Joyce has this advice for anyone just about to face it themselves.

Forget about the other people and concentrate on your own game plan. That's plenty to think about. The more focused you are the more you'll progress. Another thing you have to ignore is the rejection letters and believe me there will be plenty of those. Even if it seems you're never going to make it just keep your head down and keep going; believe and you will achieve. I don't know one single person in the business who hasn't received rejection letters – they really are par for the course. When you are rejected for a job ring up the news editor and ask them why you didn't get it, this is the only way you're going to learn. Journalists are supposed to ask questions so never be afraid to ask them!

Sport

4

Sport

To many people in the industry being a sports reporter is second to just one thing, being a professional sports person. For some it's not so much a job – more a hobby they get paid for. The BBC Sports presenter, John Inverdale, is a classic example of someone who would rather be playing it than reporting it. Every Saturday during the rugby season without fail you'll find him battling it out on the pitch for his local team, Esher RFC. Because sports reporting is so popular places in the squad, so to speak, are extremely competitive so if you want to compete at the highest level you need to display a high level of commitment.

Just as in news good sports journalists are very passionate about their work. When you're spending lots of time outside in the wind and rain a lot of passion is often required. But before you can even consider reporting on a Nationwide Conference league football game, never mind a Premiership one, most reporters have to serve their apprenticeship in the lower leagues. In an industry where jobs are limited most national reporters, if not all, will have begun their careers in local newspapers or radio. It's unlikely any national television station will even consider you unless you've got this kind of experience behind you.

As in most other fields in television work, experience is your main ticket in. Manning phones at a local radio station, collating results or reporting on local football matches for your local paper is the tried and tested way. Not only is it an excellent introduction to the craft you'll also find out whether you've got what it takes (working each weekend for no money is not everybody's idea of fun). Hospital radio stations are also good places to start. New reporters are often welcomed with open arms.

But what does it take to make it to national level? This is, after all, what many reporters aspire to. The first thing required is experience – plenty of it. In a competitive field where the opposition is formidable sound experience is mandatory. It stands to reason – the more you have the more marketable you are. The Executive Editor at BBC Sport, Philip Bernie, knows exactly what kind of experience you need. Lots.

> Experience on local newspapers or at local radio stations is second to none. If you can work here then you can certainly work at national level. It's a great training area and often good fun too. If you're already working locally then you're in the best place to be because it's from here we recruit national reporters. If you can show off an impressive portfolio and experience then there's every chance you can make it. To get your foot in I suggest you offer to help out at weekends, that kind of thing, the same sorts of methods you'd employ trying to get work at local level.

> The difficult part these days, I think, is getting the work at local level itself. Few jobs and lots of aspiring reporters mean stations are often saturated with applications. Having said that, if you're persistent and show a keen interest you should have no worries getting work. Although it may not be much to start with it's experience in the bag and that's what packs a punch in this business.

If you're at that stage where you're just about to start knocking on a few doors then be warned, don't expect to be paid. You must remember that hundreds of hopefuls are all after the same kinds of jobs so radio stations and local papers can afford not to pay you a bean. News agencies are also worth considering. No matter how big or small, most of them like to provide the best possible coverage. If you volunteer to offer your services for nothing they're more than likely to be very grateful you're there and therefore use you in some capacity. Know their coverage and be prepared to offer some idea of what you could do for them. One idea could be to go to a local game every week and offer phone reports and interviews from the ground. After that you've just got to wait for your break. It's the old adage of 'right place, right time'.

Sports helpers or 'anoraks' as they're sometimes affectionately called, usually work on Saturday afternoons. Most work at one place for a short while before taking their experience some place else where the work is more rewarding. As Philip Bernie says, it's the experience not money that should count at this stage. If you're a student then it's advisable to start getting as much experience as soon you can while you're still at college. Although it means working in your spare time the sacrifice will be worth it in the long run. That aside, you can rest assured if you're not doing it then someone else is.

The Executive Producer at Sky Sports, Andy Cairns, is also an authority on what is required to make it to national level. He appointed 50 new recruits when the station began 24-hour broadcasting. In his view, even though you may have the experience, it's important to know the industry inside out.

> I look for people who can prove to me they have a genuine fascination with the subject. What still surprises me is the number of people I interview who aren't prepared at all. Some candidates' knowledge of current sports news is scant to say the least. When you go for an interview you must always be prepared enough to be able to discuss the sports issues of the day and not just name them. Also, be ready to answer how you would cover a particular story or how Sky would cover something differently from say, another station. These are pretty standard things but you'd be surprised how many people just don't have a clue.

> Here at Sky we take on people who won't necessarily have been working in sport, some may have a great passion for the subject but have worked for a small production company. The main quality my reporters need to display is energy, and masses of

it, because when you're doing the same job all day every day then you've really got to enjoy it. You need to be passionate.

With Sky Sports now broadcasting around the clock reporters have to be able to work swiftly under pressure. Turning reports around quickly and re-writing packages in time for the next bulletin requires a special kind of person.

When time is against you and the next bulletin is looming you can't afford to panic. Sports journalism can often be very stressful and sometimes here at Sky you may find yourself producing a few reports a day. Sometimes the hours are long and they're often unsociable. If you value your weekends then maybe sports journalism isn't for you. But all that goes without saying, if you want to be a first class sports reporter you have to be willing to put that first.

With the onset of digital television more channels will mean more sport. In turn, more sport will mean more jobs. But just like the rest of television although now maybe a good moment to enter the profession you may want to consider just how much the role of a sports journalist is changing. Philip Bernie says although it's an exciting time for sports reporters it's also an uncertain time.

No-one is sure where digital TV will end up, say, in 10 years time but obviously at the moment the explosion of channels is good news if you're looking for work. On the down side I do think there's a real danger that some channels could become a sausage machine churning out the same kind of stuff and lots of repeats. The skills required of reporters may become quite basic, time consuming and maybe even technical. I don't think reporting is going to be as exciting as in the past but then that's the way television as a whole is already going. Compared to the past TV now has a much more rigorous structure and the role of your average sports journalist could become a lot more limited.

As in all areas of journalism an in-depth knowledge of their subject is vital for sports reporters. You can learn as many facts as you like from books but it will always be obvious to those in the know whether or not you have a long-standing passion for a certain sport and the knowledge that goes hand-in-hand with it. An 'anorak' may seem a slightly derogatory term for people who help out on Saturday sports shows but maybe that's the type of person you need to be to make it. Peter Drury, the ITV football commentator, travels far and wide covering top-class matches. He may have the dream job now but it's his reward for many years of hard work.

> Enthusiasm for sports reporting has got to be genuine. You can't kid someone that you're interested in sport. I think it's something you exude and you'll eventually get clocked if you're short of knowledge. The other thing is you've got to be quite hardened about the whole thing because an awful lot of people are going to say no before they say yes. In the beginning rejection is a matter of course so you've got to be prepared to deal with it.

> A lot of people think being a sports reporter is all glamour but of course it's not. I've reported from Halifax Town Football Club which is always the coldest place in the world, even in June. With no-one at the ground and the atmosphere non-existent it's certainly not glamorous. But when you do finally get a break my final bit of advice is avoid becoming cynical. Try to remember on a daily basis just how fortunate you are to be doing what you're doing. Being a sports reporter is a great job. If you don't appreciate it there are thousands of other people who will.

Before we get too disheartened at the thought of what lies ahead in our pursuit to become top-flight sports reporters just think of the competition as a race. Despite thousands of entries very few ever make it to the end. The reason is because many people don't realise just how committed you have to be. It's very much like being a professional sportsman – making sacrifices is unavoidable. If you've already considered this and are still determined to make it then little else needs to be said. Keep your eyes on the finishing line and remember that no matter what hurdles await you none is impossible to jump.

John Inverdale

On Side

"Don't expect to play in the Premiership without sampling Division Three first."

Considering John Inverdale is one of the country's leading sports presenters it may surprise many to learn he's never really had a game plan of his own. In his words he's just 'gone with the flow.' Success for John in the world of broadcasting, however, has undoubtedly been fanned by a fierce ambition to make it. As someone who always wanted to be a top athlete, being a top sports journalist was something in which he wasn't going to come second.

> For as long as I can remember becoming a major international sporting superstar was always top of my agenda. When I eventually realised I wasn't any good at it I thought the next best thing was sports journalism. The way I figured, how else was I going to get to the Olympic Games?!

John Inverdale first started putting his journalistic nous to the test while he was at University. Southampton provided the city while history provided the subject. Working on the student newspaper it was actually news rather than sport that provided him with his first foray into reporting. Straight after graduating John secured a job for a local newspaper in Lincolnshire before heading down to Cardiff. There he completed a post-graduate diploma in Journalism. It's at this point John is keen to offer his first top-tip.

> If one of the purposes of this book is to offer advice to people on how not to do things then for goodness sake take note.

The mistake I made when I left college was agreeing to let a newspaper put me through a post-grad course. Although the paper paid my tuition fees it was only on the condition I got paid half salary during my first year of work. Of all the decisions I have ever made this has to be one of the worst and as a consequence my ignorance resulted in me living in one of Britain's grubbiest flats. If some nice newspaper proprietor ever comes up to you promising you the world if you study a journalism course in return for half salary when you join his paper then under no circumstance say yes!

Although he may harbour regrets about the condition of his contract it seems John enjoyed the work itself. Parish council meetings, obituaries, stolen bikes and cats stuck up trees became familiar but amusing territory. The *Lincolnshire Echo* remained his home for two and a half years before the inevitable break was made into radio. First stop was Radio Lincolnshire before a move to Radio 4 to work as a reporter on the prestigious *Today* programme. Although he had by now reached the dizzy heights of national radio that all-important bumper pay packet was still proving as elusive as ever.

I think that's the thing about journalism, you can't expect to get paid much in your formative years. I'd been in the industry eight years before moving to London and I have to confess I didn't have a bean. I know that may sound rather precious but it's true. I hadn't been able to save anything at all as I'd hardly earned any money. If you think the streets of London are paved with gold you should think again. The only reason you should go to the big city is if you think it's the next logical step in your career. That's solely why I went.

About the same time he started at Radio 4 John Inverdale first began reporting on sports matches. Radio 5 quickly followed and he had soon established himself as a competent sports journalist. It was only a matter of time before television beckoned but when the opportunity arrived John almost blew it.

I was working on radio's *Sport on 5* at the time and one evening I was busy doing the ironing at home when the phone rang. When I answered some bloke who I'd never heard of before was on the other end and told me there was a new satellite station being set up. He basically wound up the conversation by asking me if I'd like to go and work there as a sports reporter. Because some of my mates at Radio 5 were real wind up merchants I immediately thought it was a joke so telling the guy to take a running jump I slammed the phone down. It later transpired the guy was totally legitimate and actually Nick Hunter, a fantastic fellow, from the satellite station BSB. Fortunately he phoned back again two minutes later and said: 'Do you normally do that kind of thing when someone offers you a job?!'

Despite his initial treatment, Nick Hunter repeated his offer and after accepting John Inverdale started at BSB six months later when the channel was launched. The satellite station provided John with a great training ground in television broadcasting and enabled him to make early mistakes without too many people taking note.

The great thing about working for BSB was because nobody was watching it basically provided me with free training. I was getting paid for being hopeless. If you're just starting out then I recommend you too get a job at a satellite or cable channel first. Even though the money may not be that good it will give you excellent grounding and show you what television is all about. With so many new stations starting up, now is the time to get in there and learn. If you work for a small organisation like this for 12 months then you'll be able to put yourself on the job market by the end of it.

There are concerns by some people in the industry that the mass expansion of channels we are seeing now is bringing with it a mass expansion of poorer journalism. With new reporters being paid less by stations and more airtime to be filled quality is being sacrificed. This is something John himself fears too.

I do think the standard of journalism is going down at the moment and I can see that continuing. People are getting into the industry within 30 seconds and these are the journalists who are making fundamental errors because they haven't been taught the craft properly. I think there's definitely been a shift. When I first finished college there were experienced reporters who would look at you and think, 'What the hell does he know?' and until you got to know the names of the local parish councillors then you weren't accepted into the newsroom. In a way I think that was good because it meant you didn't get ideas above your station. You only have to look around newsrooms now to see that's changed.

According to John there is also a danger of presuming that just because you are good at one medium doesn't necessarily mean you'll automatically be good at another. Television, radio and newspapers can be worlds apart.

All three modes of journalism are completely different ball games and require very different skills. I believe radio has a lot of soul whereas television is a lot more clinical. Radio is much more free and easy as opposed to TV which is more complicated and formal because of its very nature. Just because you're an accomplished radio reporter doesn't mean you're going to be equally effective on TV.

To be a good journalist it's vital to reflect your own personality and not to try and be someone else. People can see through any bull. The great broadcasters like Wogan are always the same whether they're in front of a microphone or not. They are who they are all the time. I personally don't regard broadcasters who think they're someone else with a great deal of authority.

It's interesting to hear John talk about the complexities of both radio and television and how different they are. When I first moved into local television from radio I assumed it would be very much the same kind of thing – broadcasting is broadcasting after all. I quickly found they are in fact very different and, as John points out, require very different skills. As a radio reporter you are very much left to your own devices whereas in television you have to be a team player.

The technical skills required for both are also distinct, especially now more television reporters are editing their own packages.

Anyway, let's assume you've decided it's specifically television or radio you want to try for — as jobs in broadcasting they're both equally competitive. What advice can John give to help you secure that initial break?

> For starters don't shy away from taking any job in journalism at the outset. If you can work on a weekly newspaper in Tavistock or Sunderland then within four years you could be working on Radio 4 or BBC 1. Don't think that you have to go in at a higher level, you have to play in Nationwide Division Three before you can consider playing in the Premiership. When you leave college just remember there are two or three people who do know rather more than you. Be prepared to learn from everybody and don't assume you're the next Jeremy Paxman because there's only one of them.
>
> Persevere and be patient because it's an industry that often moves very rapidly but can sometimes be very slow too. It could be you're looking for a job at just the wrong moment when there's a certain element of stagnation in the industry. My advice is bite the bullet for a year or so, stay where you are and in a year's time things will probably have changed again and people will be biting your hand off to work for them. This is how I've found it. Never take every kickback as the end of your career because it isn't.

One other bit of advice John can offer is always expect the unexpected. When you're having a quiet news day where nothing in the whole world seems to be happening, never assume that's the way it's going to stay. John Inverdale the cub reporter can confirm this by recounting one particular experience at the *Lincolnshire Echo* that left him with a bitter taste in the mouth. Working the early shift one Sunday morning it soon became apparent it was going to be one of those days a journalist dreads — there was literally no news around. Despite phoning all the voice banks, checking the wires and listening to local radio stations it appeared that absolutely nothing had happened in the whole of Lincolnshire that night, not even a bar room brawl.

Finding good stories is an integral part of a journalists job but you will find there are times when your resources are stretched to the limit. And I mean stretched! At times like this it doesn't help when your news editor is a real tyrant. My old editor at the Lincolnshire Echo had a habit of coming into work on Sunday mornings and asking reporters what stories they had. On this occasion when I couldn't find any news I was petrified at the thought of telling him I had nothing so I immediately grabbed the phone and pestered the police again. Pleading to the officer on the other end I said, 'Listen, you've got to have something for me. I can't believe that not one single incident has occurred overnight, that's just impossible.' Checking his files the constable said, 'Well, there is just one thing but you probably wouldn't be interested in it.' 'No really I am, what is it?' I replied, suddenly hopeful that I'd found a story at last. 'Well it's nothing much, just a small car fire that's all. It's really not that big a deal.' 'Listen,' I said, 'I'll take anything.' Opening his file the officer went on to describe the incident – a Mark II Cortina that had suddenly burst into flames in the early hours of the morning along Carlisle Road. 'Carlisle Road?' I interrupted, suddenly realising that's where I lived and also kept a Mark II Cortina. 'What's the registration number?' 'OHT 7OF.'

Going white at the sudden realisation that this was actually my car I slammed the phone down, ran out of the building and legged it home as fast as I could. Half a mile later when I turned the corner onto Carlisle Road there was my beloved Cortina in a smouldering heap. Police later told me the car had caught fire after a small explosion in the petrol tank. But it wasn't all bad news. The story did at least make it onto the pages of the papers evening edition!'

You have been warned! Despite life's occasional hiccups John Inverdale's managed to do all right. If you're an avid sports fan you'll know he not only hosts *Rugby Special* but also presents *On Side* the programme which gives him the chance to chat to some of the worlds most successful sports people. If you're not too envious of the man with the dream job and feel that one day you too can match his talents then be prepared to give yourself a little confidence. Apparently, that's compulsory.

> To get to any top presenting position no matter what it is you've got to have belief in yourself. Television is one job where you can't afford to be insecure. Having said that, there is also the element of right place right time, that's always the way. In the end if you're competent people are going to employ you so don't worry too much about when you're going to get noticed. It will happen. Broadcasting is a vibrant and ever changing industry and people will always need vibrant and go-ahead people. There will always be opportunities. If ever there was a time to graduate into the industry it is right now. The opportunities are far greater than they have ever been. As Arthur Daley would say, 'The world's your lobster!'.

Clare Balding

BBC Racing

"If you are in any way a prima donna then don't go into television. Carrying your own kit and getting stuck in when things go wrong is just the tip of the iceberg."

If you've seen the racing coverage on BBC Television lately then odds are you've noticed a change. Gone is the stuffy image of old and in place instead is Clare Balding, the BBC's latest sensation. The 28-year-old has joined partners with ex-champion jockey Willie Carson to present an all-new racing programme. The aim is to appeal more to the younger generation and – with a steady increase in viewers so far – the format seems to be working.

> I think the BBC knew it had to change because there were an awful lot of people who felt alienated by the old format. The average age of the racing team was closer to 60 than 40 and that isn't good when you're trying to attract a younger audience. The nice thing about me and Willie is we have developed this almost soap opera relationship and half the time people just tune in to see whether I'm going to hit him!

Clare Balding spent her early life surrounded by horse racing. Her father is the well-respected trainer Ian Balding who trains the Queen's horses. By the time she was 18 Clare had already established herself as a champion amateur jockey herself but decided she didn't want to pursue the sport professionally. Despite her contacts in the racing world Clare has had to fend for herself in the broadcasting world. Working hard to learn as much as she could about the subject, she secured her first break in radio.

> I started in radio just after I'd finished college. I was invited by the presenter John Inverdale to look at *Sport on 5* go out and ended up making the tea. Later that year my mother bumped into the commentator Cornelius Lysaght at a race meeting and he asked me into the studios again. I liked the look of what I saw and so when I was offered the opportunity to work there I jumped at it. I think what stood me in good stead was I actually turned up when I was invited in the first place. You'd be surprised how many people are asked along but then don't even bother showing up. If you're keen and you show willing then there's always a chance you'll get asked back. It could be just the break you're looking for.

Although Clare's own enthusiasm helped her get the job it was soon tested. Despite being given the chance to work on the race reports there was still a small price to pay. The bulletins started early in the morning, 5.30 am to be precise, and the pay was lousy. The test was whether she'd last the course.

> When you're getting up at around four in the morning for a minuscule wage of just 100 pounds a week it can be a trial. I think what kept me going is the fact I was getting experience and the more experience I was getting the quicker I could move up. Let's face it, no one's going to pay you loads of money with no experience so there's no way around it. Luckily, after a short while Radio 5 offered me a trainee sports reporter post that meant more money and relatively normal hours. It couldn't have come at a better time because I was exhausted and broke. I actually started my new position the very first day Radio 5 Live went out on air in April 1994.

Clare was lucky because the position she was offered was created especially for her. Before then Radio 5 Live had never hired anyone as a trainee sports broadcaster. The producers admitted that this was their chance to mould someone into the kind of sports reporter they wanted. As a raw recruit Clare received the traditional treatment and was thrown head first in the deep end. She remembers her first bulletin well.

> I was terrified. I was so nervous in fact I raced through the whole bulletin as fast as I could to get it over with. The only point where I slowed down was right at the end when I announced the racing results. As it was a subject I was comfortable with I just relaxed. Straight after the bulletin had finished the Head of 5 Live at the time, Jenny Abramsky, came downstairs to see me. 'That wasn't bad.' she said. 'If you can make the rest of the bulletin sound just like the last minute you've got it made.' 'But I didn't relax until the last minute.' I answered. 'Exactly.' she replied.

Throwing yourself into a new job is often a good idea. What isn't advisable is finding solace on the telephone to friends. Clare found this out the hard way.

> I've always had a habit of being on the phone and I was on it a lot when I first started mainly because I didn't really know anyone. One time though I guess I pushed it too far. It was when the daytime producer caught me talking to my friends yet again. Completely losing it she screamed at the top of her lungs, 'Never have I known anyone so unconcentrated or so untalented get so much airtime!' She's actually a very good friend of mine now but did teach me the art of concentration!

After learning the basics of radio Clare's break into television came not long after in 1995.

Passing a screen test she was asked if she'd like to work on the programme *Rugby Special*. Soon after she found herself on a plane to Atlanta to work on the Olympics. Reports on show jumping and skiing followed. It was only recently that Clare was asked to take over from the racing presenter Julian Wilson after he suddenly announced his retirement. Since then rising to challenges has been a continual campaign.

> I think to begin with an awful lot of people thought I was far too young and far too inexperienced for the job. At the start

the age thing does slightly count against you and I know the BBC took an enormous risk by offering me the job with so little experience. When Julian announced he was retiring I didn't think I was ready to take his place at all. I was a 26-year-old woman who hadn't really proved herself in front of the camera. To put me with Willie too, who was equally inexperienced, really was pushing the boat out. Still, as the former England coach Glenn Hoddle said, 'If you're good enough you're old enough' and I really believe that.

Although it may seem like a simple transition, switching from radio to television often takes some adjusting. When a viewer can put a face to a voice many presenters find they are far less forgiving.

If you make a mistake on radio then you can get away with it. If you cock up on television you're taken to task more. The general public can be very unforgiving. You have to be thick skinned because sometimes you get the occasional letter that is negative. I tend to ignore them because at the end of the day as long as your employers are happy with you then that's the important thing. As much as the general public are important, if I'm only getting a couple of weird letters from an audience of three million for a programme like *Grandstand* then I'm not really too worried.

Another aspect of television is being able to think quickly on your feet. When a video tape gets jammed in the machine and a producer starts yelling for you to fill time, two minutes can seem more like a lifetime.

When something like this happens you've just got to remain calm and relaxed, you can't let on to the audience that you're filling. With no scripts or prompt to read from you just have to busk it and I usually go over the results of the day again or give a synopsis of what's to come. Of course that's all easier said than done and drying up can be a problem. I think ad-libbing becomes easier the more you do it and I know what's stood me in good stead is being the president of the union at my old university. I used to do a lot of public

108

speaking in front of an audience so that was good practice. If you get the chance to do that kind of thing yourself then go for it because it definitely builds up your confidence.

As if that's not enough on the occasions when you do think you've done a good job you may not always be commended. When you're presenting then praise can be a rare commodity.

> Television can be desperately lonely. It's no wonder there are so many insecure presenters around because no-one ever tells you whether you're good or bad. If you're bad then you're just taken off air. It's difficult to stand back after a programme and assume you're good because it's such a subjective medium. It's not like when you're a lawyer and you can commend yourself after winning a case because television is not that black and white. You have to make yourself not need to hear compliments from other people. That's difficult.

Despite the hurdles she's had to jump herself, Clare has managed to stay ahead of the field. For a young woman who started presenting on television with little or no experience that's quite a result. Although she only began her broadcast career a few years back people are already asking for her advice.

> People are always coming up to me and asking me how I got into broadcasting. My reply has always been the same, 'I can tell you but I don't think it will help you.' The reason is because no one person ever does it the same way. My only advice is decide first what area of TV you want to go for before you pursue it. Different fields require different approaches.

The other important lesson is never under-estimate what it really takes to make it in broadcasting. In the beginning working anti-social hours is standard and if you're expecting a king's ransom for your efforts then you can forget it. Only once you have established yourself will you begin to be paid well and that often takes a number of years. A lot of people outside television have this view that because the industry is so tough to break into then the chosen few who do manage to crack it are rewarded by ridiculous salaries. The only ridiculous thing about starting salaries is how small they are. This is why you have to love the job.

> You've really got to want to be in television because that is the only thing that's going to motivate you in the beginning. The pay certainly isn't. Another home truth about TV is that job security is not great. A lot of people are working on contracts if they're lucky as there are hardly any staff jobs any more. There's also lot of travelling and your parents are always going to ask, 'When are you going to get a proper job?' If you're going to do any sort of journalism you've got to find something that to some extent you're an authority on. Knowledge of a certain sport helps. At the end of the day if you find your niche then you're going to enjoy the job more and if you enjoy the job more you're going to be better at it.

Even though she's still a young broadcaster, for all her experience Clare is no longer a novice. Despite a hectic 12 months she's still managed to keep her head up and prove she can run with the best of them. This isn't always as easy as it looks. But even at the tender age of 28 Clare knows people can have too much of a good thing.

> With me the tide is just starting to turn, I can feel it. I know I've been on television too much recently. It's the classic thing of over exposure, people get bored of seeing your face so they start to pick holes in you. I don't mind criticism though because it's inevitable. If you're a presenter you've got to expect it. In the end I think it's small price to pay because there aren't many jobs around that match working in television. If you can get past the first few years there's no better profession.

Gary Newbon

ITV Sport

"Television is like golf, just when you think you've mastered it you drive straight into a bunker. You've got to keep your concentration at all times, even at the highest level."

Gary Newbon has a lot to be happy about. At 54 years of age he's already celebrated 30 years in ITV Sport, no mean feat when you consider how dramatically televised sport has changed recently. With six World Cups under his belt, three Olympics and hundreds of world title fights many young journalists can only dream of emulating his success. But according to Gary, dreams can easily be turned into reality.

> I consider myself to be one of the luckiest guys alive. Not a morning goes past when I don't wake up and think how privileged I am to be doing what I'm doing. But it doesn't seem that long ago when I was just a young apprentice myself. I remember thinking then that all I wanted to be was a national newspaper reporter. Looking back now I'm glad I didn't settle for that. I'm proof that if you think bigger you can achieve bigger.

Gary Newbon's meteoric rise up the ranks of ITV Sport began in 1968. He was offered a job at Westward Television (now Carlton TV) in Devon working for the sports desk. He knew the company would provide an excellent training ground. Then he moved to

Birmingham. Billy Wright, who was head of ATV (now Carlton TV) in Birmingham, was looking for a new face to present the sports news. Gary knew it was an opportunity he couldn't pass.

> After making all my mistakes and learning what makes good television at Westward I felt I was ready to take on a new challenge and environment. That's when I went to ATV. I think it's important to set yourself challenges because that's how you move on. But when I first got to ATV I couldn't believe how basic the set up was there, it really needed changing. So, with the help of a presenter called Trevor East, I set about improving it.

Some people argue that the difference between those who make it further in life and those who don't boils down to standards. Although most people are content with what they perceive as good there will always be those individuals who strive for better. In the end it's the latter who travel further. According to Gary this philosophy is vital if you are to get anywhere in life.

> If I tell one of my reporters to get an interview with someone then I really expect them to get it, I always have and I expect the same. If you're pushy enough then you can get anything, literally anything. Reporting is all about being demanding, if you don't get an important interview then your rival just might. That's the way you've got to think in this game you've got to think one step ahead all the time. That goes for the rest of life too.

It was newspapers that first attracted Gary's attention when he was 19. Although as a keen sportsman he knew he wanted to be a sports writer, he thought it was a good idea to start in news first. You'll find that many other top sports presenters started their careers in the newsroom too. Not only does it provide an excellent grounding in journalism, it's often said that if you can work in news and current affairs then you can work anywhere. This aside, with sports reporting becoming even more specialised and competitive it's often advisable to start in news first then break into sport only after you have established yourself. In the beginning Gary worked for a variety of sports agencies providing copy for major newspapers. Working obsessively, within a year of starting he'd quickly made it to senior reporter. This sort of drive and determination to ascent the ranks quickly became a familiar force throughout his career, but he's had to work for it.

Only once you've stepped through the doors of a television studio does your journey begin. If at that point you think you've made it then you're sealing your own fate. The first thing I had problems with was nerves. One time during the early part of my career I worked with an old boy called Kenneth McCloud who presented the news. I used to sit next to him and read the sport. In the beginning I kept complaining how my nerves kept getting the better of me and all the time he'd tell me I shouldn't worry. Naturally, that was little consolation.

Then one day he came into the studios and told me he'd thought of a way to cure my problem. I asked him what it was but he told me he'd tell me later. That evening I was getting ready for him to hand over to me as usual for the sport news. In those days when he had finished there was a 20 second break before the camera came to me. On this particular night, as soon as the break started, he suddenly leant over, grabbed me by the testicles and squeezed as hard as he could. I winced in agony and was just about to voice a few expletives when the break finished and the camera switched to live. It sounds ironic but it was one of the best bulletins I had read to date. I was in such shock that I completely forgot about my nerves and as a result looked more natural.

The second thing Gary realised he would have to make more sacrifices. As any presenter or reporter will tell you, there's no avoiding them. Whether it's night shifts, being on call 24-hours a day or working weekends, unsociable hours are an integral part of a journalist's life.

In the beginning making sacrifices was difficult. I can't tell you how many times I've had to miss important family events but there's no way around them. There are no cutting corners in this business as it's not a nine to five job. When you're just starting out you have to accept them. To get yourself through the hard times I think it's important to use something to drive you on. I use my family. At the end of the day as long as I'm providing them with the best things in life then that's a good enough reason to make sacrifices.

Gary first broke into television by writing off to all the local TV stations. Where possible he arranged to meet as many sports editors as he could. In this business putting a name to a face is crucial so it's always wise to follow up speculative letters with a meeting. It also shows willing! Although most of your initial inquiries will inevitably be met by the standard reply – 'Thank you for the interest you have shown in this company, we will keep your letter on file' – never let this stop you arranging a meet. Once you've impressed sports editors with your effort you'll find it a lot easier to get through to them in the future.

As is often the way, although Gary Newbon at first received the usual sack full of rejections, one particular week he got a call from two different stations. Westward and Anglia were looking for a junior sports reporter. Working in newspapers had provided Gary with a great grounding in journalism and for him a junior sports position in television was the next logical step. Passing both interviews he decided to take the Westward job for what he now says was the wrong reason.

I went to Westward, as I mentioned earlier, because I foolishly thought I could get away with making more mistakes down there. With the station based in Devon I figured if I screwed up in the beginning then when I finally left no one at another station would know. Of course thinking back this is stupid because no matter where you work you're bound to make mistakes to start off with. Not only that but the business is quite a closed shop anyway so people will always know how good you are. Reputation precedes you. If I had my time again I don't think I would worry about the mistakes I made quite so much. Everyone makes them and that's the way you learn.

When most young reporters start work, especially in television, surviving the initial few weeks can sometimes be a challenge. Not only do you have to work in an alien environment with strange technology, you sometimes can't help thinking about the thousands of other people desperate for your job. The pressure is on. Gary has this advice for people just starting out.

> When you begin in television it's like going down a dark tunnel. Everything seems totally strange and you wonder whether you will understand the language – VTR, graphics, script terms and so on. I remember when I first started I honestly thought I'd get the sack. I was scared out of my wits and kept thinking everything I did wasn't good enough. I got it totally out of proportion. Of course, you can't keep thinking like that and after a while I shook myself out of it but it's not easy. In the beginning you've just got to keep your head down and work hard – putting in extra hours if need be. This builds up your confidence and shows people that you're committed. Starting in television is like learning to drive, skate, ski-jump and swim all at the same time. Although it's impossible to master them all at once, within no time you'll soon be on top of things.

In the beginning it also helps to know that most people already working in the business started their journey from exactly the same place as you. That knowledge is comforting in itself. Although the road to success won't always be straight you can rest assured the further you travel the easier it gets.

> It's understandable why some presenters and reporters look scared and frozen like rabbits caught in headlights when they first start out. When you're a presenter the camera lens can seem cold and cruel. It gives you nothing back, no encouragement, no interest and it doesn't smile or laugh at your jokes. Just try talking to a window to see what that's like and how long you can keep going. Eventually, with time,

the lens becomes your friend and your confidence will have grown so much that you learn to become a performer. In a way presenting is about acting in front of the camera. The more confident you are the more people at home will trust what you're saying.

Once you have established yourself you must never get complacent. In an industry that can hire you then fire you before the contract has even dried it's also important to keep your contacts.

To get on in television you must make people believe in you. You not only have to work hard to achieve this but you must be loyal to people, especially those who have given you a break. Integrity is one of the ingredients of success so never stab anyone in the back. I can honestly say that in 30 years in the business I have never done anyone over and that's important to me. In the end it means you get people batting for you. If you're to succeed in this in this job you need the support of others.

Although Gary Newbon admits he has had an element of luck getting to the top of his field, one thing that has guaranteed his position is his determination.

I think determination is one of the great secrets of life. Believe that and you'll go far. Of course, when you're first trying to break into television you must also do your homework. It's worth putting in time studying the best people and talking to the best people. This way you'll know what it takes and what to aspire to. We're moving into a new age of programming now so learn about digital television and what it will mean in the future. If you want to be on top of a specialised subject like sport, you have to read about it so scan the papers and Teletext regularly. I don't want to over dramatise it but television is one of the best professions and you've got to earn your position. Anyone can break into TV if they're determined enough but your ultimate goal should be to make it to the top. Just remember, people who don't try for the premier league won't make it to the premier league.

Jill Douglas

Sky Sports

"Adopt Nadia Comaneci's approach to life... always be prepared to be flexible!"

If you're hoping to carve out a successful career in television then Jill Douglas knows just the tools required. Forget relying on pure luck or the odd contact to propel you forward, if you want to work in broadcasting you need to display bags of confidence and even more enthusiasm.

> Unfortunately, there's no room for shrinking violets in this business. If you're going to be a good reporter you need to be confident. I'm not saying you have to be confident in a self-centred way but just strong enough to push yourself forward. When you walk into a room you've got to be able to go up to the people you need to talk to no matter who they are. In this job it's no good settling for just anyone at the back of the crowd. You have to thrust yourself to the front if you want to interview the right people. Enthusiasm is also essential. Few editors will want to employ you unless you're keen and willing to learn.

The same can be said for getting that first job in television. If you don't apply yourself then you may find that initial break remains elusive. The buck doesn't stop there either. When you do finally start working in TV the pushing has got to continue. If you're going to make it to the top of your field there's no way around it. Jill Douglas can verify this. She hasn't made it to Sky Sports News by waiting patiently on the sidelines.

> You have to go for it a 100 per cent. I'm not saying you must sacrifice everything in return for a career but there should

be times when you are totally focused. Take my career. There are periods when I'm completely focused and put other things to one side. You don't have to live all your life like this but for certain periods you have to cut everything else out and concentrate on your work. Those key moments when I've knuckled down have always paid off. At the same time I'm also a firm believer in having other interests, you can't shut yourself off permanently.

Jill Douglas is one of Sky Sports latest recruits and her career first began in 1988 in Scotland. Aged just 17 she turned down an opportunity to study politics at Edinburgh University for a job at her local newspaper instead. Jill was employed as a junior reporter at *The Southern Reporter*. It was the kind of job she had long dreamed of.

I can't remember precisely when I decided to become a journalist but it was at a very young age. Before I sat my 'O' Levels a local paper offered me a job because I was forever banging on their door for work experience, hanging around the offices and generally pestering them. I turned it down at the time because I wanted to study my highers for a place at university. I actually come from a farming background so I don't know the reason why I became interested in reporting – it's just always been my ideal job. When I finally completed my exams *The Southern Reporter* offered me work and said they'd put me through journalism college. As journalism was something I was determined to break into I decided to go for it. I couldn't think of a better way of learning the craft than actually doing it.

Jill took a diploma which was recognised by the NCTJ (National Council for the Training of Journalists.) An NCTJ course is widely regarded in the industry as one of the most prestigious a journalist can study. There is also a separate diploma for broadcast journalists. Working in newspapers gave Jill a great grounding in news reporting and taught her the ropes from a reasonably young age. Choosing this route rather than university is something she's never regretted.

Someone phoned me recently to inquire about the best way of breaking into broadcasting. I told them the best way was to start by learning the trade in local newspapers. I believe there is no substitute for it. I honestly think that what I learned in newspapers has stood me in great stead for the rest of my career. I not only learned how to find information but was also taught the ethics of journalism. Many people who float straight into broadcasting now without a newspaper background don't understand how things work. Working on a local paper or local radio station gives you a great grounding and shows the importance of checking things out.

After newspapers Jill worked in the Edinburgh bureau of *The Daily Record* and leap frogged radio straight into TV after a chance meeting with Border Television's Head of News at a press conference. She obviously impressed him because days later when she bumped into him again he offered her a job on the spot. Jill started as a sub-editor before taking a career break and spent time in Africa. When a year had passed it was back to Border and in late 1992 she was taken on as a full-time reporter. An opportunity to present also arose.

I was given the chance to front the early bulletins and thankfully after three months they realised mornings weren't my thing. After that I reported and presented the news in the evening on the magazine style programme *Look Around*. It was great because it has the biggest audience and is hugely popular in Border TV land.

It was during her time at Border that Jill first became involved in sport. Presenting a rugby programme called *The Union and the League* she also reported on sports matches for the main news programme. A few years later she met the producer of BBC's *Rugby Special* when BBC Scotland was looking for a new presenter. The same producer called her up and asked if she fancied screen testing for *Rugby Special*.

I thought it was hilarious because to me the programme represented the last bastion of male broadcasting. After a successful screen test I was offered the job. I was taken on as a reporter and presenter for *Rugby Special* in Scotland but I also worked for BBC radio too.

As a female at the helm of a male orientated programme Jill proved it isn't impossible for women to break into mainstream sports presenting. Although she may have had to fight her corner a little more than her opposite numbers she showed that if you're good at the job then there's nothing stopping you.

> Being a female sports presenter isn't seen as terribly novel anymore. I look at the people I work with now and there are a lot of women. From the very first day I started on *Rugby Special* and even before that at Border no one has ever questioned why I was working in sport. The only time somebody has said something is when a football manager once asked me, 'Why are you asking me questions about football, you're a rugby reporter aren't you?!' Obviously you have to know what you're talking about but that applies as much to men as it does women.

After being suddenly catapulted into the realms of national television one other consideration for Jill was the pressure to perform. It doesn't matter what gender you are, when you're a presenter on mainstream television the only thing that counts is whether you can work as part of a team.

> What fazed me when I first started presenting was working on my first OBs (outside broadcasts.) When you work on big events there are hundreds of people involved from electricians and PAs to cameramen and producers. You can't help thinking, 'My God, if I screw this up I'm also screwing up the efforts of everyone else.' It's slightly overwhelming. As a presenter you need to take one step back and consider how important all these people are. They're all professionals so it's vital to do your job well.

Reflecting on her career thus far Jill is more than content with her lot. Travelling down to London to start work at Sky has proved to be the right move. The decision to work in sport will never be something she regrets because there aren't many other jobs that offer the same benefits.

The overriding advantage of doing what I do is not having to worry about it once the day is over. It's not like working in news, which I believe is more stressful. Once you decide to move into sport I don't think there's any real way back into news so it's the kind of decision you need to weigh up.

When I first started as a journalist it wasn't a conscious decision to become a sports broadcaster. I actually enjoyed news a great deal and was involved a lot in politics during my last couple of years at Border. If I hadn't gone into sport I would probably have stuck with politics, particularly now there's so much happening in that field up in Scotland. I've been lucky in that people have offered me jobs at just the right time. I guess it proves an element of luck does come into the equation in this type of business.

As we've heard before there's no harm in creating your own luck either and the way to do that is to start getting as much experience as you can. The more experience you get the more people you meet and the more people you meet the more likely someone will notice you. As Jill will confirm it only takes one person to give you a break and you're increasing the odds of that happening if you're in a working environment. Not only that, there's never a better time to enter television than right now.

People are desperate for information and new TV channels are creating an explosion of jobs. There's still a shortage of good sports reporters and if you're keen to learn properly and not too eager to run before you can walk then you shouldn't feel daunted by the prospect of working in TV. You should embrace the challenge and be excited by it. That's the whole thing about television isn't it? You've got to enjoy what you're doing.

There's no magic formula which determines whether someone breaks into television. That's down to the individual. What I can recommend is learn as much about the industry as you can by talking to people already working in it. Believe it or not most are very accommodating. The hardest bit I'd have to say is getting your foot in the door and how you go about that is up to you. I got offered a job at a regional newspaper by hammering on the door and I broke into television by impressing a news editor I met at a press conference. It's different for everyone. Keep pestering is always good advice and try to avoid becoming depressed if you feel you're not getting anywhere. Breaking into broadcasting is not something you can achieve overnight, it takes a while. Keep your head down, keep going and you'll eventually be rewarded with a break. Be determined and I can guarantee it.

Children's TV

5

Children's TV

Everyone knows it takes a lot of tenacity to break into TV and children's television is no exception. If a producer were given a penny each time they heard someone say 'I want to be a children's TV presenter' many would now be in early retirement. But although it is a difficult field to break into it's certainly not impossible. If you've got talent, you're persistent and refuse to lose sight of your goals then there's no reason why you can't make it.

Still, no matter how high our aspirations lie, we could all use a little help now and again. With this in mind I have enlisted the advice of three of the industry's leading figures. As experts in children's television they know exactly what is required to make it. The first, Chris Bellinger, is Head of Entertainment at the BBC. Working at the Corporation for almost three decades, Chris has been a major force in shaping Saturday morning television. Responsible for producing heavyweight programmes like *Going Live!* and *Live & Kicking* his knowledge of the industry is second to none.

> Obviously the competition in children's television is enormous but that shouldn't put you off. Every other field in the industry is exactly the same. As long as you keep your head down and remain focused then a career in television is not unfeasible. If you're good and you're committed there will always be a lot of opportunities for you, especially at the BBC. For a start we cover a wide range of programmes that require different kinds of presenters. The secret is to target your niche.

This is a good point. When you're first starting out it's imperative to work out what kind of programme you want to work on and where you want to aim for. As digital television sets in there will probably be an even bigger choice in the future. Once you have decided, then try to learn specific skills required for that kind of presenter. But what kind of experience do producers expect the presenters of tomorrow to have?

> I have always said that hospital radio is a great way to get into television, it's a tough environment and very good training ground. If you can work at a radio station like this it shows you can get on with people. This is crucial because television is all about being a team player. Hospital radio also introduces you to presenting and it's here you will find out whether you've got the talent for it. Once you've got this kind of training then you should try for work experience at a TV station.

Work experience is one of the best ways of getting your foot in the door. Working at a station for a few days gives you the perfect chance to show just what you've got. Although the daily tasks may only amount to opening letters or manning the phones you still have an opportunity to stand out. The important thing is to exploit it. One man who knows a lot about work experience is Executive Producer, Graham Douglas. He was the person responsible for launching CITV and has seen hundreds of youngsters help out at the station.

> I know some people may turn their nose up at unpaid work experience but what better way is there of showing a producer what you're capable of? I personally look for initiative — people who can work on their own and find constructive things to do. You'd be surprised how many people come to CITV and just sit there for the whole week doing nothing. One thing is to come up with new suggestions for the show. Although they may not be taken on board they demonstrate a person is genuinely interested in the programme. Getting ahead in television is all about

130

getting ahead of your competitors. Always think what you can offer that they already haven't.

The other good thing about work experience is it will help you decide whether you actually want to work in the industry. It's helpful to know these things early on. It will also give you the chance to see the various jobs within television. In children's TV there are a lot of researchers or PA's (Programme Assistants). Researchers are responsible for bringing new ideas to the show, helping with scripts and building contacts. A PA's role involves organising contracts, copyright clearance and legal work. Working as either gives you the opportunity to experience children's television first hand and can eventually lead to greater things. Many of today's presenters started as researchers or PA's themselves.

Of course there is no point trying to break into children's television if you don't know much about it. If you've never heard of programmes like, *SMTV, Mad For It* or *Wise Up* then you had better start wising up yourself! Only by knowing about the industry are you likely to get ahead in it. One of these programmes has won a BAFTA award; the question is which? If you don't know the answer then you should really ask yourself just how serious you are about a career in children's television. It's this kind of question that could well be asked in an interview.

As far as presenting is concerned, if you've already decided that's what you want to go into then it's time to act. The first thing you're going to have to create is a showreel. A showreel is important because it not only shows a producer what you look like – it also illustrates what kind of personality you've got. This is important because different programmes require different personalities. The Commissioning Editor of Children and Young People at Channel 4, Andi Peters, is an expert on showreels. In his job he tends to come across a lot of them.

> In my experience the worst thing you can do is make a showreel too long, the ideal length is a couple of minutes. Producers want to see how natural you look in front of the camera and how relaxed you are so try to enjoy yourself. If

you can, try to interview someone on your showreel because it's important to see how you react with people. This is not always as easy as it looks. Finally, just be yourself because that's the only way you're going to demonstrate your personality. At the end of the day this is what a producer is looking for, a certain person with a certain kind of flair.

Andi Peters has a wealth of experience in children's television. Some of you probably remember him presenting in the broom cupboard on CBBC. He also produced the popular pop magazine show, *The O-Zone*. As a presenter, producer and commissioner he's certainly the person to ask what it takes to make the grade in children's television.

> You need an inordinate amount of persistence if you want to get ahead in this game. Thick skin too is also an advantage. Because it's a competitive industry you are bound to get rejections at first no matter how talented you are – but don't let that deflate you. You've just got to keep going. I think it takes a special kind of person to make it in television because even if you are good you have got to learn to cope with rejection and disappointment. Not everyone can, so the few that make it certainly get my respect. My advice is always keep a vision of what you want in front of you and don't get too disheartened by the knockbacks. They happen to the best of us and I can vouch for that.

Just as in every other field in television, such as news or sport, supply will always outweigh demand in children's television. When CITV advertised for its two presenters more than a thousand people sent in showreels. Imagine trying to whittle that down to the last 50. With this in mind it's important to produce a good CV and show tape as it's these two things that will determine whether you get selected for an audition. The showreel doesn't have to be made by an expensive production studio, more often than not a simple camcorder will do. The CITV presenter Danielle Nicholls can back this up. Without her auntie's camcorder she probably wouldn't have got the job. Graham Douglas, CITV's Executive Producer at the time, was one of the people who had to trawl through the plethora of showtapes that landed on the mat. How does he determine who would make a good presenter just on the strength of a showreel?

> Intelligence, sense of humour and presence are very important and are things I can pick up on a show tape almost at once. Some people may have one or two of these qualities but I need all three. Presenting may look easy but in reality it's a very demanding job requiring wit and the ability to think on your feet. The links at CITV aren't pre-recorded and the presenters don't use an autocue, it's all done live. Imagine what that takes? I don't look for good-looking girls or good-looking boys either, I look for someone who has instant charisma with whom the viewer can warm to.

Scaling the mountain of success may take a lot of climbing but reaching the summit is not impossible. Although there will always be times when you lose your footing and you feel you're getting nowhere you've just got to keep your head down and keep going. But why take it from me? Here are four of the country's most talented young presenters to tell you more.

Margherita Taylor

T4

> "People who achieve are the ones who are given an opportunity and take it. People who don't are the ones who are given an opportunity but don't see it."

Although a regular nine to five job may sound tempting, if you're planning a career in television then you can forget it. You can also forget free weekends. Success in TV has a price and that is working unconditional hours, there's just no way around it. The radio and TV presenter Margherita Taylor can vouch for this. Even though she's now established herself as one of the most exciting new presenters in the country she still faces the prospect of unsociable hours.

When you're working in broadcasting there's no such thing as a normal job. A 14-hour day is not unheard of. I've had people in the business tell me they haven't had a day off in two years and I believe them. You've got to understand that in this business crazy hours are a permanent fixture. Its not just in the beginning of your career either. The more successful you are the more hours you put in. You can forget going to Ibiza with your mates, it just doesn't happen. You can't afford to plan time off ahead in case you get offered work that week.

There's no bitterness when Margherita tells you this just an acceptance. As she said, in broadcasting working unsociable hours is standard. Her current weekly schedule is a good example. As though working on the BBC children's show *Electric Circus* and Channel 4's youth programme *T4* wasn't enough, she's also got regular Saturday and Sunday slots on Capital FM. Oh, I forgot to mention, she also presents a sports and entertainment show called *No Balls Allowed* which is now in its second series. How does she fit it all in?

> You just have to. Although working more hours means less time to yourself it's something you've got to do. If you don't then someone else will. Besides, I'm not complaining. I love what I do and it is totally worth it. Broadcasting is definitely the business to be in.

Margherita Taylor first knew she wanted to work in the media before she hit her teens. Ever since that moment everything she has ever done has been geared towards turning that dream into reality. While studying for a Media and Communications Degree at the University of Central England, Margherita gained work experience at MTV, Choice FM radio station in London and at BBC Pebble Mill in Birmingham. Although she received no payment she knew she was getting valuable experience in the bag. In the beginning of your career this is worth more than money itself.

> If you're trying to get your foot in the door work experience is the only way in. Let's face it, no-body's going to offer you a job if you don't have any. Trying to get work experience in broadcasting is also a good way of finding out what it's like to get a proper job in the industry too. It's tough. I don't know how many times people have come up to me complaining that they keep getting rejected just for work experience. I feel like telling them, 'Listen, if you think it's difficult getting work experience just wait until you get to the real world where you do have to pay your way.' I've always said that if you can't handle the rejections at this stage then you've got no chance of making it. You might as well just forget it.

Margherita managed to land her first job not long after finishing university. One day she spotted a 'Search For A Star' competition in her local paper in Birmingham. The contest invited budding radio presenters to turn up for an audition with the winner earning the chance to present a weekend night show on BRMB. Margherita couldn't resist.

> I dragged my friend along with me and for an hour we queued on a cold Sunday morning waiting to be auditioned. There was a long line of people and I couldn't help feeling we were really out of place. Everyone else looked like your typical local radio DJ if you know what that type looks like. When it finally got to my turn I was asked to talk about myself for one minute, introduce a record, read the travel and then read the weather. It was a nightmare. For a start I thought I'd screwed up the travel and I knew for a fact I'd pronounced a couple of names wrong. You can imagine how surprised I was when a week later I got a call telling me that I'd won. I couldn't believe it.

As it happens, the director at the station wanted a fresh voice and Margherita provided just the sound he was after. The weekend night shift she was offered quickly turned into the weekend breakfast show and Capital FM soon offered her a night shift there. As the number one commercial radio station in London this was a proposition she couldn't refuse. It was about this time she also embarked on her TV career. It was a classic case of being in the right place at the right time.

> It was when BRMB staged the 'Search For A Star' competition again the following year. I was still working at the station and this time a TV crew came in to film events. As part of the programme the director interviewed me about what it was like to win the competition and how it had changed my life. I knew it was a chance to gain experience in front of the camera so I gave it my best shot. Two weeks later I got a call from the same guy who told me he was so impressed with my interview that he wanted me to screen

test for another programme he was making. I agreed and got the part.

The production called *Heartland* was commissioned by Carlton Television and broadcast around the Midlands. For Margherita the programme proved priceless because it soon led to other things. For a young lady who was used to working mostly on the radio TV soon became familiar ground. But although it may have been a lucky break which got her the *Heartland* part it was pure persistence which landed her a job on *The Clothes Show*.

When I was 21 I went to see the editor of the programme. I've always wanted to present on *The Clothes Show* so I thought I might as well try my luck. Unfortunately, it didn't go too well. When he found out I didn't have much experience I was promptly told to go away and not to come back until I had got some. Although I was disappointed I phoned him up periodically in the ensuing years just to let him know I was still around. Then, five years later, I went to see him again. This time I was armed with the experience he wanted so he couldn't really refuse! I think persistence is a wonderful weapon to possess in the fight to get on in the media. You certainly won't get very far without it.

Persistence and commitment are admirable qualities but if you want to compete in the broadcast industry then you'd better get used to something else. Plain old hard work.

I think lots of people who want to get into this business think it's going to be an easy ride. They read about certain celebrities having a wild time in the press and just assume that is what it's like all the time. How wrong they are! What they don't realise is that these same people are also working extremely hard, sometimes unbelievably hard. Not just that but before they got to where they are today they will have had to put in tremendous hours working every shift going.

Presenting can be hugely exhausting, both mentally and physically. The stress is also something people don't realise.

When you're first starting out it can sometimes be worrying just wondering whether you can afford to fill the fridge with food.

Although the road to success is difficult it need not be lonely. OK, so it's up to you to motivate yourself and provide as many opportunities – that goes without saying. But if you look in the right places there are always people willing to help you out and that in itself can be encouraging. One good idea is to choose a mentor, someone who can guide you and advise you along the way. Usually this person will be someone who is successful themselves.

> The majority of people who succeed love seeing that in other people. They love seeing someone who is as hungry as they were when they first started out. More often than not they're only too happy to give out advice, after all they know how difficult the industry is. They will also respect you more because the fact you are asking questions means you want to get on. My advice is hook up with someone you admire and ask them to give five minutes of their time. They can tell you the key things about getting on. Listen and learn.

Learning is not just confined to the beginning of your career. Margherita says even today, after years of experience, she's constantly learning too.

> Everyday is a challenge and a learning experience. Some days after I've had a bad show I sit myself down and mentally go through exactly what went wrong and how I can improve things. I think you've got to do this. Although at first I feel like I'm useless and that I'm no good at anything, I eventually get a grip on myself and work things through in my mind. If you can honestly learn from your mistakes then there's a good chance you won't repeat them. This is important because if you do repeat them then it means you're not learning at all. You'll find that people at the top rarely repeat the same mistake.

One mistake in broadcasting is not having a game plan. It's not only important to know where you want to go but how you are going to get there. Lack of planning can result in lack of progress.

> I think it's vital to have a plan of action. Most successful people all have a plan and they don't give up until they reach their objectives. When you reach one objective then it's time to set another one. This is how you get ahead in business. Also, just because you suffer a setback doesn't mean you should totally re-think your strategy either. In the media there are always going to be setbacks and rejections, they're par for the course. One thing I quickly realised in this business is you're pretty much on your own so you've got to rely on your own self-belief to get you through the hard times. At the end of the day, when everything else seems like it's falling apart, it's only self-belief that's going to keep your head above water.

The philosophy behind success is simple, what's not so easy is making it happen. But the point is, if you are really motivated then you can literally make anything happen, even in television. Here's Margherita with some final advice for the budding presenter.

> If you're looking for a job but haven't yet found one then make yourself more employable and stock up on more ammo. If you want to be a TV presenter on *Blue Peter* then learn to ride a horse or learn to trampoline. If you want to work on a programme like *The Really Wild Show* then learn about animals. If you want to be a journalist then take up shorthand or master another language. Getting ahead in broadcasting is all about selling yourself. If you can do that then you're virtually there.

Kirsten O'Brien

Children's BBC

"Focus on your own ambitions and forget the competition. Faith in your own ability is what really counts."

W hen people ask Kirsten O'Brien what it takes to break into children's television her reply is quite simple, 'Where do you want me to start?' It's not that it's difficult to explain but just so many people do it in so many different ways. One thing Kirsten is certain of is the kind of person you have to be. Apart from talented, to make it as a children's TV presenter you've got to be very very committed.

> I think you've got to be really willing to put yourself out – especially when you're looking for that first break. When I see people come to the BBC on work experience I always know which ones will stand the most chance of making it. They're the one's who stay late in the office and leave when the rest of us leave. You'll be amazed at the number of people who visit on work experience and come five o'clock that's it, they're out of here. Working somewhere for a week is an opportunity to show you're willing and keen. You've got to show you're genuinely committed.

At 27, to say Kirsten O'Brien has come far is an understatement. Working on national network television is no mean feat. When you consider she's already managed to squeeze in a media studies degree and a trip around the world then it makes it even more remarkable. The key to Kirsten's success is hard work. If you want to follow suit then be prepared to knuckle down.

Nothing comes easy in life especially a career in television. I often think some people don't realise just how hard it is or the kind of commitment it takes. Before you even begin to consider entering TV it's wise to ask yourself whether you're going to give it your best shot. In the beginning there are always going to be obstacles to deal with and you've got to be sure you can handle them. Some experiences are not going to be very pleasant at all.

One major experience many people find hard to deal with is rejection. Not only can it drain your self-confidence in one fell swoop it's also responsible for a high proportion of people giving up altogether.

Everyone has failed auditions, in fact I don't know one person who hasn't. The trick is to turn rejection into a positive thing by learning from it. When you get rejected for something then ring the producer up and ask them why you didn't get the job. It could be because you didn't look relaxed enough or because you were too over-the-top. These are things you can easily remedy, but if you don't ask then you will never know. Find out whether you can watch a copy of your audition and ask the producer what areas you can improve on. They know how tough getting a job is and many are usually only too happy to advise.

Rejection was something Kirsten O'Brien had to face herself when she was first chasing her dream. One audition in particular left a deep impression on her mind – quite literally.

I was invited to try out as a presenter for the BBC Education Department. I'd got to the second stage of the interview process so my hopes were quite high. The job itself would be quite physically demanding with the presenter involved in different activities each week so because of this the audition was quite active too.

Taken to a nearby swimming pool all the interviewees were told that part of the test would involve capsizing a canoe and rolling it back over. Unfortunately, when it was my turn to capsize, as I didn't have much experience in this kind of thing I cracked my head really hard on the bottom of the pool. It was quite painful to say the least. Although I managed to somehow get the canoe back up, I felt very sick and a lump the size of a marble began to appear on the side of my head. Later that same day on dry land, the next test was demonstrating terminal velocity with three pieces of plasticine. Concentration and communication were the key skills needed for this but because I felt so sick I could hardly focus on anything never mind the plasticine. My performance was less than perfect to say the least and in the end it transpired I was actually suffering from concussion. Needless to say I didn't get the job!

Kirsten always knew from a very young age that what she really wanted, more than anything, was to be a children's TV presenter. As soon as she turned 15 she began working towards that dream. Joining a local hospital radio team in her native Middlesborough, Kirsten's first encounter with broadcasting was working on an opera show. Although she wasn't allowed to read anything on air (or sing) it did give her the chance to learn the ropes. In radio this meant finding out how to monitor levels, how to record material and how to edit on a reel to reel machine. Working on roadshows and seeing live broadcasts injected her with even more determination to work in television. It's the live element she loves the most.

There are so few programmes that go out live these days and I think I'm so fortunate to be able to work on one of them. The thing about live TV is it's so exciting and the buzz it gives you is indescribable. I really believe that if you can work in live television then you can work anywhere because it takes every kind of skill.

After studying for her 'A' Levels, Kirsten travelled to Birmingham to take a Media and Communication Studies degree at the University of Central England. The year was 1990 and at the time there were only about five other courses of its kind in the country.

For my first year I had to do a third of the Government and Political Studies degree because Media Studies on its own wasn't yet recognised. I took the course because it was practical. I learned how to edit properly, found out how a studio works and I was taught the basics of broadcasting. If I had studied say, an English degree or a subject like it, then I would have had to concentrate on writing essays and as a result not learnt a thing about what I really wanted to work in, broadcasting. If the course you're studying doesn't contain practical elements then my advice is try to get work experience at a radio or TV station and learn things that way. You've got to know some basic skills before you can expect people to take you on. I did my radio placements at Piccadilly Key 103 in Manchester and Metro FM in Newcastle and learned a great deal.

After her full-time education was finally over Kirsten got the call to go travelling. But just before she left she managed to secure four weeks work experience when she returned. The place was Tyne Tees Television in Newcastle. Her mum's friend had seen an advert for a local newsreader in *The Daily Mail*. Knowing where Kirsten's ambitions lay she had dutifully sent it to her.

I filled out the job application form at Gatwick airport! It was a real rush job and one of the most made up application forms I've ever done. I was quite shocked when I got an interview. The job was reading the early local news bulletins and in the interview a panel of five people fired questions at me. I also had a screen test. I'd never even seen an autocue before let alone read one. That night I got a phone call from the News Editor who told me that although I hadn't got the job because I wasn't experienced enough, they wanted to offer me some work experience. I was delighted because it meant I could still go travelling for a while.

When Kirsten arrived back home she knew it was time to get her head down and work hard. She had already managed to get her foot in the door of a TV station so it was important not to let the opportunity pass. Her initial first four weeks consisted of everything from making calls to researching stories and when her time was up she offered to stay on at the station and help out for nothing. Making herself as useful as possible her hard work paid off when a newsroom assistant left two months later and Kirsten was offered his post.

> I really do believe that if you want to work in this industry there comes a point where you have to work for nothing. There's no way of avoiding it. Here at CBBC our runner started from a stint at work experience and although it may seem annoying that you don't get paid anything you've just got to accept it. If you stick at it then it will be worth it in the long run. When I got offered a job at Tyne Tees I was soon allowed to report and from that I was able to produce a strong show reel. I also used to stay late at night and read dummy weather reports and bulletins in the studio. I wouldn't have been able to do any of this if I hadn't worked for free first.

Kirsten spent two happy years at Tyne Tees and while she was there she literally got to try everything. One of her favourite jobs was presenting the weekly *What's On* slot. But although she enjoyed what she did she never once lost sight of her real goal. Subsequently, she used time off work to set about achieving it.

> I had two week's leave coming up so I thought, 'Right, you can't let your dream of becoming a children's TV presenter just float away so you're going to have to go for it now.' Staying late at work I shaped my show reel into exactly the kind of thing I thought a children's TV producer would look for. Then I bought 50 blank VHS tapes and after copying my show tape on them I mail-shot every children's producer in the industry. The next step involved travelling down to London to try to meet them but unfortunately, when I got there, the trip didn't turn out to be very productive. Most of the people I wanted to see weren't around. Slightly disappointed I headed back up north but when I got back home there was a letter from CBBC asking me down for a

chat. Excitedly, I prepared as much as I could for it because I knew this was a big chance.

When I eventually turned up I thought the chat went horrendously. I didn't feel entirely comfortable and I don't think I managed to get across the real me. A week later though I received a letter from the producers inviting me back for a screen test. I knew this was my last chance to shine. When the big day finally arrived I gave what I thought was a great performance and I remember saying to my mum it really depends on how other people at the screen test got on because I truly felt I hadn't put a foot wrong. In the end my performance must have been ok because I was offered a job. It just goes to show that even if one part of a test or interview goes wrong you should never give up.

Because CBBC gets so many showreels sent to them it's extremely rare they advertise for presenters. If they like the look of one then they'll ask the person in for a chat. If that goes well then an audition usually follows. Because of this it's vital you produce a good showreel. According to Kirsten a good show tape should be no longer than three minutes and should demonstrate the real 'you'.

A showreel can be absolutely anything so long as it shows your true character. In the end you can't really lie about who the true you is so don't pretend to be someone else. I recommend interviewing someone on a showreel and include a section introducing yourself. Like I said, you can literally do anything. The BBC presenter Toby Anstis changed the wheel of a car on his – now you can't get much more boring than that! Apart from producing a good showreel the other thing is to learn as much as you can about what's happening in the industry. Know how it's changing and what programmes are on air. The amount of people who don't know these things is quite staggering so make sure you're not one of them.

Working in live television involves an incredible amount of preparation and when she's not on screen then Kirsten is usually getting ready for a show. Although she's been at the BBC for three and a half years now Kirsten still thinks she's incredibly fortunate. When you're doing a dream job there's not many people who take it for granted.

> I often used to think that maybe I came into children's television too late. I definitely think that if I'd left it any later then that would have been pushing it. Then again I loved doing my degree and when I went travelling that was just brilliant. You have to do whatever works for you. I think as long as you keep focused and try to do as much as you can along the way to make yourself more employable then that's good. My one bit of advice is never ever give in. When you meet an obstacle learn from it but don't let it put you off altogether. Being a television presenter is a dream job and there are often days when I still can't believe I'm doing what I'm doing. When you get people like Philip Schofield coming into the studios and telling you he's never enjoyed anything more than his time at CBBC then you know you have to make the most of every second.

Richard McCourt

Children's BBC

"If you don't have a vision of where you want to go then you'll never get there."

Picture the scene: a nervous 19 year old walks up to the gates of BBC Broadcasting House and just before he enters he pauses for a second. Looking up at the famous pebbled wall it suddenly dawns on him that everything he has been working towards during his whole life has been geared to this moment. Haunted by the realisation that the next 30 minutes will determine whether he lands the job he's always dreamed of or take him back to square one he walks on… the audition awaits him!

Now this may sound like an epic drama straight out of a 19th century novel but it's actually a real-life scenario all young presenters face. There's no escaping the big audition. When you've been working hard at something for as long as you can remember and you finally get a chance to prove yourself you can imagine the pressure. The 19 year old above was actually Richard McCourt himself just three years ago when he was invited to try for a presenting job.

> I remember the day well. It was nine years after I first decided I wanted to go for a career in children's television. When I got to the front of Broadcasting House it struck me that the pressure was on. Here I was about to try for a job I had wanted to do all my life and whether I got it or not would all be decided in the 20 minutes which preceded it. I was terrified. The strange thing was, however, that although I was extremely nervous my fear quickly disappeared the

moment I started the audition. It was almost like fate because it was the first time my nerves have suddenly vanished like that and as a result I gave my best performance. Consequently, here I am at the BBC today.

Although going for an audition is a major test in itself, just managing to land one is equally tough. Because most producers don't advertise for new presenters it is up to aspiring presenters themselves to secure an audition. This isn't always so easy. To get one you must prove to a producer that presenting is something you're serious about. They'll want to see evidence you've been working hard to try to make a go of it. Take Richard McCourt for instance. He first started working towards his presenting ambitions when he was 12 years old. While his friends were still playing cops and robbers and kicking a football around Richard was already formulating a plan on how to become the next Philip Schofield.

It's difficult to explain but from a very young age I always knew that TV presenting was the only thing I wanted to do. My older brother was an influence because this is something he was interested in too. He's actually two years older than me and currently works as a presenter on the Disney Channel. When I was very young nothing other children of my own age did interested me as much, I was always pretty focused on making a move into television. It was like a bug had bitten me and I was infected for life, it just never went away.

If you were to examine most of today's top presenters you'll probably find that they too were bitten by the broadcasting bug at an early age. It can be highly infectious. For people like this there is no cure and this is why they just have to keep going for their goal – it's in their blood. For other aspiring presenters, who have been bitten by the same bug but with less severity, the rejection letters and knockbacks that follow usually provides the perfect antidote – they give up. Commitment is compulsory if you want to make it at anything.

When you write off to a producer hoping for an audition they are looking for one thing: whether you're totally serious about what you want. They'll want to see how long you have been trying to break into the profession and what experience you have to back up your application. If you've only just finished college and fancy taking a stab at presenting a producer will see straight through that almost immediately. You need some kind of experience. I started at the bottom in hospital radio and that's the best place to begin. Firstly, you'll find out whether you like it and secondly you can begin to expand your CV. That's very important in this business.

Sheffield Children's Hospital was the place Richard first started in the broadcasting business and he ended up staying there for eight years. The hospital radio broadcast to around 200 children and proved a popular station. At 12 years old Richard was the youngest person the station had ever employed in the 15 years it had been running.

Although I spoke with a high voice I managed to prove to people at the station I could present on radio. After that things proved less difficult. It also became slightly easier when my voice broke after I'd turned 15! At hospital radio stations people want to see whether you fit in with other people there because broadcasting isn't just about presenting, it's a team effort. Companies like the BBC will also want to see if you're a team player and easy to get along with. This is an important element if you want to succeed.

While he was working at his local hospital radio station Richard studied a media course when he was 18. Drama and English were also on the agenda. The crunch came when it was time to decide whether to continue going for his presenting dream 100 per cent or go on to university instead. He decided to put the latter on ice for a year until he'd at least had the chance to go for his goal.

I'm very fortunate in that I have very supportive parents and they helped me out a lot when I was younger. After I had finished a B-TEC in media studies I decided a whole year of getting as much experience as possible was important. My attitude was to go for it and if things didn't work out then I could always go on to college the following year. My first job was working on the magazine *TV Hits* reviewing singles and the latest movies. I also got a job at Capital Radio in London and helped out at a big event of theirs at Earl's Court, back stage stuff. Basically it was just being keen and getting as much experience as possible for my CV. Unpaid work shows people how committed you are to getting a paid position in the industry. Everyone has to do it.

In the meantime, Richard was fortunate to be able to produce a good showreel himself. His hospital radio team had just bought a new video camera and was busy setting up its own amateur television studio. After borrowing the camera to interview famous celebrities in Sheffield and shoot his own links, Richard had soon perfected the kind of show tape he knew would catch a producer's eye.

When I was happy with my showreel I sent it off to every single TV company in the country, literally everyone. I counted on most people sending it back but the big shock for me was when the Nickelodeon channel returned my tape saying I wasn't right for their kind of style. I was equally shocked when CBBC wrote back offering me an audition there. As one of the biggest and most prestigious stations in the country it was brilliant. It just shows there's no accounting for anything in this business. Although I got rejected by a smaller satellite channel I managed to land a job at a main terrestrial one.

Naturally, rejection isn't the most pleasant of experiences but we can at least squeeze something positive out of it. Richard made sure he phoned or wrote back to every single producer who rejected his applications and asked them why they didn't like his tape and how he could improve it.

I was moving house not long ago when I stumbled across five folders full of rejection letters. There must have been 500 of them. I've got so many I could wallpaper my new house with them. Some replies were from when I was 13, 14 years old from places like Radio 1 and ITV stations. The fact I've got a job at the BBC now proves it doesn't matter if you get turned down at one place you should still keep trying. Producers and styles change all the time so never be afraid to apply to the same place again six months down the line.

If you think that the difficult part is just becoming a national television presenter then it's worth considering this also when you're in the public spotlight you have to accept that in reality life is not always as straightforward as it seems.

> You must realise that being a presenter always poses challenges. The competition to get in some place like the BBC is big but once you are in here it gets even bigger. There are so many new presenters these days on so many channels that the pressure to perform is always there. Sometimes you might see a different presenter getting a better job than you and you think why? Then if people stop saying you're doing a great job all the time you can start to question whether you are any good.

> Another disadvantage is you can't bring your worries to work. If you have an office job then at least you can hide behind a desk to a certain degree and keep yourself to yourself. You can't do that in my line of business. If you've had an argument with your partner or you've got a bad hangover then you've still got to act like you're on top of the world. This can be difficult. If you don't act like you're in a good mood on television viewers can tell.

So, still interested in being a TV presenter? If you are then one consideration appears to be the pressure to perform doesn't stop when you eventually land that big job. On the contrary, as Richard says, the pressure to do well always remains high. This is probably something not many people consider. If you still think you've got what it takes to follow in someone like Richard's footsteps then here's some more advice from the presenter himself. The first concerns showreels and, ideally, what you should be putting in them.

For my showreel I introduced myself saying who I was, where I came from and briefly what my interests were. After, I interviewed a few interesting people from a local fête that was happening in Sheffield at the children's hospital. This kind of thing shows a producer if you can talk to people in a natural way and whether you can control an interview. Try to speak with a local celebrity if you can too. The rest of my show tape comprised film reviews and competition run-downs. I don't recommend anyone copying what presenters actually do on CBBC. Producers like to see you for who you are and to come up with novel ideas for your showreel. At the end of the day bosses will know whether you're being your own self. They don't like people who mimic what they see on television.

It's important to realise that all presenters go through bad patches and belief is the only thing that gets you through them. If you're an aspiring presenter yourself then you must use belief to pull you through the bad times as well. When you've got a dream in front of you, you just have to think at the end of the day that if you want to do it and you think you can do it then you're going to do it. There will always be other people out there who you think are better than you but they may not have the same determination. Lots of different elements are required to make it as a national presenter not just one and you need all of them to succeed. You have to want the job 100 per cent. If you want something bad then you're eventually going to get it.

Danielle Nicholls

Children's ITV

"Nobody owes you any favours, you're basically on your own. The only fuel that's going to propel you to the top is your own belief."

When you meet 20 year-old Danielle Nicholls the first thing that strikes you is her energy. She has masses of it. To begin with you wonder where she gets it from then, when you start speaking to her, you realise the energy stems from her enormous determination to be the best. For Danielle being the best is the only option.

> I've always tried to excel at everything for as long as I can remember. I'm pretty competitive and if I like doing something then I don't enjoy being second best. It's not that I want to beat everyone else around me, just I don't accept it when I don't give something my best shot. It's a cliché I know but that's the way it is. If you're going to do something then you must insist on giving it a 100 per cent. Life's just too short to accept anything less.

It's refreshing to meet someone so young with such strong views, but after you get to know Danielle you realise she's had to grow up quickly. Leaving school after her GCSEs to study a BTEC Diploma in Performing Arts meant Danielle had to deal with disappointment early in life. When you're aiming for a competitive and often heartless industry like entertainment then living with rejection is something you have to get used to.

> There are lots if instances when I have had to deal with disappointment but one particularly unpleasant occasion was when I auditioned for an all girl band in Manchester.

The former manager of *Take That* Nigel Martin-Smith was organising the auditions and was looking for five girls. When I turned up I was feeling really positive. I felt in good shape because my voice had been coming along well. Because I was so confident, when it was my turn to sing on stage I gave what I thought was close to my best performance. After the audition Nigel came up to me and told me I'd done really well, but if I hadn't received a phone call at home that night then it meant I hadn't got a part.

It turned out to be a very long night and while the clock ticked the phone remained silent. Willing it to ring didn't help either and by 11 o'clock a heartbroken Danielle resigned herself to the fact she'd been rejected. What made it worse was she thought she'd come so close.

To say I was devastated was an understatement. I just couldn't believe it. I think I cried practically all night and the next day there was no way I could face going into college.

Although she spent the whole of next day in bed Danielle told herself she had a choice. She could either take the rejection and use it to make her stronger or let it get her down. The latter she knew would get her nowhere.

I realised quickly that in this business you can never afford to take things personally. Just think about it. If a producer or director already has an idea of the kind of person they want then there's nothing you can do about it. If they want a blonde when you're a brunette what are you going to do, dye your hair? You can't afford to feel sorry for yourself in this game. What I've learned instead is you've got to turn the disappointment around to make you even stronger. Rejection should stoke the fire of determination even more.

Learning from the experience is exactly what Danielle did and keeping her head down she went on to complete her performing arts course at Oldham College. Dance is one of the things she loves most in life and, after finishing college, she joined a pop group called *Pure Gossip*. The group was a dance troupe based on the seventies funk masters *Hot Gossip* and it gave Danielle the time to improve both her singing and dancing. It was also time for her to meet her first big challenge, professional rivalry.

> There were a couple of people in the group who I didn't get along with but one girl in particular caused me real problems. Not only did she try to bring me down all the time there were occasions she'd play mind games to try to dent my confidence. It seems funny to say it now but if I saw her again I think I'd shake her hand and thank her because she's partly the reason I've made it this far. She hurt me so much that that at the time I vowed I would never give up in television until I'd made it.

This particular experience hardened Danielle to the harsh realities of entertainment and has stood her in good stead. Now when someone gives her a hard time she literally just let's it pass. Danielle knows she can afford do this because she's got something that will always obliterate any obstacle she encounters – belief.

> Don't get me wrong, I'm not the kind of person who knows I'm going to get what I want, I just believe that. I'm a real grafter and don't accept anything until I have given it my all. I count myself as pretty good at giving things my best shot so when I set myself a challenge quite often I achieve it. I guess that's what belief is – having the confidence to believe in your own abilities enough to make them reality.

Danielle's first tentative steps towards stardom began at the age of ten. Joining a dance class she soon got into the swing of things. Ten is quite an old age to start dancing and because of this Danielle found herself way behind children of her own age. Placed in a class of five-year-olds it was up to her to work her way out. Straight away Danielle displayed her iron determination to be the best and within a year she was soon dancing with her peers. This wasn't all. At 17 she went on to become the All England Dance Champion, this despite entering dancing so late in life.

I'm definitely a hard worker, I wouldn't be where I am today if I wasn't. People sometimes assume that it's luck that's helped you to the top because they don't see all the hard work you've put in to get you there.

While chasing their dreams a lot of people don't escape a taste of life on the dole and so it was with Danielle. Breaking from the dance group *Hot Gossip* meant she was suddenly out of work and two months of unemployment followed. But even during these dark days her systematic belief continued to shine through and never once did she even consider giving up.

Signing on was a pretty low time but I've always believed you've got to experience the bad to appreciate the good. I also think you have to make certain sacrifices in life if you want to realise your ambitions. When I was on the dole I never once thought of taking the easy way out and getting a nine to five job that would pay for the nice things in life. No way. I decided I could do without those things if it meant waiting a little while longer and getting better. I'm extremely lucky because I have very supportive parents who have always stood by me and shown total support. I can understand when people give up because they may not have the financial support from their parents. That's difficult and in that situation it's hard to follow your dreams. I count myself very lucky for having such support. The good thing about being on the dole was the spare time meant I could go for the kind of jobs I really wanted. I went for every audition.

And so it was with CITV. As soon as Danielle saw the advert in *The Stage* magazine for two new presenters she knew she had to apply. Armed with her aunty's camcorder she set about the task of producing a short show tape for the producers to watch. Sitting on her parent's couch in Manchester she recorded a 30 second tape of her life history and at the end, in typical Danniesque fashion, shouted at the top of her lungs '…so just give me an audition!' It worked.

I couldn't believe it when they asked me for an audition. I just screamed! I wasn't sure whether I'd actually get asked because I thought that maybe my performance on video may have been a little too over the top. It just shows that you've got to go for everything even if you think you have no chance.

Before the audition at the CITV studios in Birmingham Danielle prepared thoroughly. This seems one thing the presenter takes very seriously. While others may take the short route, Danielle leaves nothing to chance. Making sure she's totally prepared means giving herself every chance to succeed. Sometimes it seems to be human nature to skip over things we think we already know — but how wise it is to go over them again and again just to make sure. This not only makes sure we're fully prepared for an audition or interview but also gives us more confidence in our abilities when we do take the test. This extra helping of confidence can often give us the edge over our competitors and in an audition this is priceless.

Getting rid of your nerves before an audition is very important. If you're nervous then you're not 100 per cent focused on what you're doing. You've got to feel relaxed and have fun. What I always do is sit down in a room by myself and take loads of deep breaths for about ten minutes. This really helps you calm down. While I'm doing that I mentally go through what I'm going to say and how I'm going to act. Once you've managed to clear your head then you will perform much better.

This psychology seems to have worked because two weeks after the audition Danielle found out she was the new face of CITV along with her new co-presenter, Stephen Mulhern. What made her success even sweeter was until that date, Danielle hadn't had much experience in TV let alone present on it. In the end the producers at CITV received more than 900 showtapes and although a lot didn't make the grade the producers say some of them show great promise for the future. As far as the future's concerned for Danielle, right now she's just happy to keep her feet well and truly on the ground and make CITV a complete success.

I've got no other option but to keep my feet on the ground otherwise I'd get told off from my mum and dad. Besides, there's no point getting too excited as there's still a lot more I want to do. You've got to remember your attitude shouldn't change just because you've finally made it onto the screen. One thing I'll definitely be doing is working just as hard because there's no way I want to be working by the time I'm 60.

Just because you make it to the stage Danielle has reached doesn't mean you've made it. When Danielle herself first started presenting on CITV there were all sorts of new challenges to be met. As a new convert to television one of these was getting used to the studio set up - when you're working in live television everything is not as straight forward as it seems.

My first week at CITV was a nightmare. Not only was I extremely nervous – sometimes I kept muddling my links up. It's never worth taking anything for granted in television because it can be dangerous if you do. You've always got to be prepared for anything. This is what I leaned when if started working in TV almost immediately.

Rather than let the new challenges she had suddenly encountered defeat her, Danielle once again set about beating them. The very next week she studied her lines even harder and took copies of her days' performance back home to study. Sometimes she would watch them over and over again well into the early hours of the morning. Eventually her hard work paid off and as her confidence returned her performance improved.

It's a situation which you can either fight or allow to defeat you. For me, because I knew I had got so far, there was no way I was going to lose. When you've worked hard all your life for something getting close isn't good enough. I would have put in a 24-hour day if it meant getting it right.

With her career well and truly on track it's now other people who are asking Danielle for advice. Drawing on her own recent experiences she has this to offer.

I have always said there are three golden rules you must follow. The first is the most important and one you should never ever question – self-belief. The second bit of advice is always try and make the knockbacks make you stronger. If someone questions your ability then work doubly hard to improve it. Number three is always give everything your best shot. If you're not satisfied with something then it means you're not giving it all. I'm afraid in this business that's not good enough.

Entertainment

6

Entertainment

There's no set rule which says how you should break into television presenting, as each interview in this book illustrates. If there were you can bet your bottom dollar everyone would be doing it. If one thing ought to be written in stone, however, then maybe it should read: be yourself. According to those in the know, if you try to be someone you're not then you stand little chance of making it.

The best people to speak to about personalities on TV are producers. They are responsible for finding new talent on television and know what works. One Executive Producer with the BBC is Kieron Collins. He produces the *Midweek National Lottery*, *The Mark and Lard Show* on Radio 1, and also programmes for the digital channel, *BBC Choice*. Before his arrival at Broadcasting House just over a year ago Kieron worked as an independent television producer at Granada TV.

> The people who make it in television are the ones who bring a talent to the screen, whether it's dancing, singing or acting and can then cross over to presenting. Think Cilla Black, Bruce Forsythe and Michael Barrymore. The one thing that's vital if you want to survive once you make it is personality. Having character is important because you can't rely on just your talent to keep you at the top. Most people discover whether they've got a strong character when they're reasonably young because they will refuse to give up.

I get showreels that come through the post every week and 90 per cent of them are truly dreadful. People seem to think that the only thing you need to be as a presenter is loud and wacky. That's wrong. What I want to be able to do when I watch a showreel is to sit back and be entertained by somebody's personality. The best thing someone can do with a showreel is present themselves. Crazy camera angles and shouting loudly just covers up what you should be reflecting on screen, your true personality.

The same applies to covering letters. Whenever I see a wacky letter that is full of words in bold italics then I just switch off. That kind of letter is really off-putting. I'd much rather see a sensible letter that's well written and with the occasional joke thrown in. Despite what people think about television, I don't like things that are in your face. TV will always attract people who have wacky personalities but having a wacky personality in itself is not enough.

Aiming for mainstream television straight off is a difficult task so, as with news and sport, it's often a good idea to go for cable or digital programmes first. Look at the facts. Not only are there greater opportunities but you may get the chance to work on more than one programme. With small budgets researchers, producers and presenters on digital television often work on a number of shows. If you're able to reflect a variety of experience on your CV it shows you're adaptable. As a presenter, what also helps, is if you target a specific niche in television. If you can establish yourself in one area first there's every chance you can expand into other programmes later.

The *Tomorrow's World* presenter Nick Baker is a good example. Rather than a scientific expert Nick is actually an authority on wildlife and it's in this area he first developed his career. All his life Nick has been mad about animals and while he was at university he started *The Bug Club*. Organising talks and trips to see the local wildlife it wasn't long before he was writing a column for his local paper in Devon. Regional TV work was next followed by national radio and finally network television. He's already completed one wildlife documentary series on Channel 5 and has another in the pipeline. Nick's wildlife knowledge coupled with his own 'on the hoof' style of presenting is what has helped him achieve his goals.

> I think it helps if you find an area you are passionate about then target that. For me it came naturally because I have always been interested in bugs! You should be looking to start from the bottom in broadcasting before working your way up because you've got to establish your niche. I started in local papers and radio before I got a break in national television. Even then I worked as a researcher for a year just to get an idea of what TV is all about. The strategy for me was to knock on as many doors as possible and then keep knocking. You'll find that a lot of the doors don't open and the one's that do will often shut again. Just keep going.

Nick has also made a name for himself through his own style of presenting. No matter what programme he fronts his personality always shines through. If you've ever seen him on television you'll know that he never usually works to a script and is a natural at playing to the camera. His aim has always been to 'bring the adventure back into wildlife' and you can tell he's very passionate about the subject. If you want to emulate his success in this or another field then you too need to be passionate and be yourself. I know it keeps cropping up and again and again but it's important to reinforce the point, your own personality is what counts.

Paul Ashton, an independent producer with 'Libra Films' in London, can back this up. After recently spending three years in the United States he says some of the best presenters start in one specific area first before expanding into others.

> Many presenters I work with who are experts on certain subjects often find that they're quite good in front of the camera and so decide to concentrate more on TV thereafter. The classic example is a man called Fred Dibnah, a typical Yorkshireman. Years ago Fred was featured in a documentary about demolishing chimneys and was so wonderful in front of

the camera that he's made a successful career out of presenting ever since. He usually fronts programmes about industry and his persona really is unique. It's difficult for me to say how someone should be break into television but it always helps if you're an authority on something first. No matter what you're talking about, if you're good in front of the camera it will show.

One other consideration aspiring presenters are forced to realise is the importance of agents. Although they take around 15 per cent of your earnings it's them who can find the work. Acting as sales people, good agents can often negotiate better rates of pay than presenters who represent themselves. With most presenting work confined to London, if you don't live there then it's a good idea to secure one. You need someone to act on your behalf. More importantly, it's the agents who have all the contacts. As with everything in life if you're going to get an agent you might as well get a good one. The best advice is to check with Equity first before you sign with one. They're able to tell if an agent reputable. At the end of the day your career is in their hands so make sure it's a reliable pair.

All things considered, you can get as much advice about television as you want but putting it into action is up to you. What helps is to know what kind of programme you want to work on. If you haven't discovered a field you're particularly interested then you need to find one. As we've just heard, you need to be passionate about something if you're hoping to make a mark in it. Knowing your target before you take aim is vital if you want to score high.

Barry Norman

Film Night

"The most important thing in television is to tell the audience the truth as you see it. Viewers are much more intelligent than people in TV realise. If you're not honest with them they'll know."

Some would argue that Barry Norman is to movie reviews what Robert De Niro is to the movies themselves – a class act. Mind you, having reviewed films for almost three decades he's had plenty of practice! Although Barry recently moved to Sky where he currently presents *Film Night* he is best remembered for his work with the BBC. Joining the organisation in the early 1970s he was asked if he would front a new review show called *Film 72*. It was such a success he continued to present the programme for the next 26 years. In the end he missed the series just once when he went off to present the programme *Omnibus* for a year.

> Although *Film 98* marked the last series for me at the BBC I still look back on the programme with pride. I love television and *Film 98* gave me a lot of opportunities as a journalist which is also what I love. Interviewing, creative writing, trying to give a balanced account of things, they're all up there. These sorts of things are what reporting is all about.

A young Barry Norman first ventured into journalism when he was 17. After passing his 'A' Levels he worked on a weekly newspaper in

London, the *Kensington News*. South Africa was his next destination where he spent two years writing for various newspapers. On his return to London he headed straight for Fleet Street, the heart of national newspapers where he became the editor of a gossip column on the *Daily Sketch*. Climbing his way up to Showbiz Editor on the *Daily Mail* it was time to encounter his first major knockback.

> It was when the *Daily Mail* and the *Daily Sketch* merged. Half of the editorial team got made redundant and regrettably I was on the hit list. My initial reaction was one of despondency. I figured how could they do this to me? I'm much too good to be made redundant! It was hard to swallow. Then I became angry and I think this was the best thing that happened to me. I thought 'Right, enough of feeling sorry for myself. I'm going to show these people they've made a huge mistake letting me go.' And I think I did.

Spurred on by his inner anger Barry worked hard in all manner of jobs for the next year. One of the highlights was working on *The Times* newspaper as a TV critic and showbiz interviewer. He also wrote a weekly satirical column for *The Guardian* which dealt with politics and current affairs. The 12 months eventually culminated in *Film 72* the programme that launched his television career. Looking back now Barry firmly believes all bad things happen for a reason.

> When I was made redundant it was naturally an unpleasant experience but it did make me want to work harder over the ensuing months. When you work harder more opportunities arise. I think a lot of good can come out of adversity if you knuckle down but you must be prepared to work hard.

Before journalism Barry's ambitions lay in the movie business. His father was the legendary director Leslie Norman who produced classics like *Dunkirk* and directed *The Cruel Sea*. Barry wanted to follow in his footsteps. Unfortunately, by the time he had finished school the British film industry was in one of its many declines. So, after a heart to heart with his father, he decided to go for his second interest, journalism.

When I first started as a journalist I soon discovered that if you delivered copy at the required length and at the time agreed then you were already ahead of most of the competition. There wasn't as much talent around as I had first feared. If you're just about to start in the profession yourself then I'd say if you're prepared to knuckle down you've got a pretty fair chance of succeeding. When I started in television I found that a little harder because if you want to do better than adequate as I did then it gets difficult. I found I had to put more time in and assess the work I was doing. Even now at Sky my attitude is exactly the same, always to seek improvement. My aim is always to make my next programme better than the last. I may not always succeed but at least I'm trying and in this game that counts for a lot. I actually hate watching myself on television but I make sure I dutifully go through a recording of my programme every week to find out what went wrong and how I can improve things.

Yet again in black and white, here is confirmation on what it takes to succeed. Just as everyone else in this book has testified success lies within yourself – *never take your best as good enough*. Of course life at work doesn't have to be this way and you will always have the choice of taking the easy option. In work this means being satisfied with an average performance. However, as with most things in life, this choice comes with a price. An average performance results in an average job. Which one do you want?

Success takes hard work but it's not as hard to be better than the next person as you may think. Although there are a lot of journalists in the business doing well, I have discovered a lot of them are not particularly good. There are very few talented reporters out there who are willing to work at it. When I first started freelancing myself I soon discovered this and I found it very encouraging. If you're better than not particularly good then you're already ahead of the rest. Imagine what you can do if you try that little bit harder still?

Working as a film critic has enabled Barry to travel the globe to interview some of the world's greatest actors. Perhaps it is meeting such talent that has encouraged him to work harder at his own. But even though he may be experienced at interviewing the stars there is no room for complacency. Not in television! This he discovered when he met Robert De Niro for an interview a few years back. Although he is probably one of the greatest stars still shining in Hollywood, De Niro is not renowned for being the easiest person to talk to. As many American film critics can testify, if asked the wrong 'kind' of question the actor can be easily upset. Barry Norman met Robert De Niro just after the actor had finished filming *Goodfellas* in 1991. Warner Brothers called Barry up and told him De Niro was prepared to do just one interview in Britain and that Barry was the person he wanted to do it with it. Reluctantly Barry agreed.

> Knowing how difficult he could be I was a little hesitant but I was promised by Warner that he'd be full of conversation. We arranged to meet at London's Savoy Hotel but things quickly got off to a bad start when he kept me and the crew waiting for an hour. His excuse was he had been waiting for his shirt to return from the dry cleaners but if you'd seen the drab thing he was wearing when he turned up you found that hard to believe. When he walked into the room he wasn't much interested in meeting anyone. Grudgingly he introduced himself to my producer and me but didn't bother saying anything to the crew.
>
> As we started chatting it became clear he really didn't want to be here and as usual started giving monosyllabic answers. This is what he's famed for. The interview went on for about 20 minutes and when we finally came off air he suddenly got up from his chair and said, 'You had to get that one in didn't you? You just had to get that one in?' I didn't know which question he was referring to and told him so but he continued accusing me of asking him a sneaky question. As he walked off I followed him into the reception and asked him again what question he didn't like but he kept saying,

'You know which one I'm on about, you know which one.' In the end I suddenly lost it myself and squaring up to him I said to his face, 'What is your ******* problem?!' We both snarled at each other for a couple of minutes but eventually calmed down and it finally resolved itself quite amicably. That was the only time I've ever interviewed De Niro and I can tell you it was quite an experience!

The other time Barry's resolve has been tested during an in interview was when he talked to the late Sir Richard Burton. It was when the actor was coming to the end of his career and was known to like a drop of the hard stuff. Flying to Milan for the interview, Barry talked to Richard on the set of his new film. Things began well, briefly, but just as Barry had started asking his third question there was the unmistakable sound of snoring. Looking up from his notes the film critic saw that the legend was fast asleep. With his chin rested neatly on his chest it was obvious that Richard was out for the count. Quietly getting up and putting it down to experience Barry decided to chat to him the following day instead!

No matter how experienced you are there's no accounting for the unexpected. Although they say you should never work with children or animals it's fair to say some adults should carry a warning too. The great thing about interviewing someone is that one person is never the same as the next. That's exciting but means you have to prepare. It also means there's little room for complacency. If you haven't prepared for an interview then you run the risk of losing control. As a reporter it is up to you to lead the interview and search for answers. If you don't have knowledge about the subject you're asking about then what chance have you of getting to the truth?

Another problem Barry encountered in his early days was criticism. As soon as he had moved from newspapers to television he became a popular target. Although it's something that's not easy to accept when you're first starting out it's something you quickly have to learn to live with.

The problem I have is everyone thinks they're the best film critic in the world. You go see a movie then you're a critic.

It's because of this a lot of people hate me for doing a job they feel they can do better. A lot of these people work for newspapers and magazines and know nothing about the medium whatsoever. In the beginning some of the comments made about me got to me because you know that there is a personal motive behind them. But after a while you realise that they're usually just fuelled by jealousy and you learn to push it out of your mind. If you're a presenter you must remember that you're doing a job thousands of other people would kill for. You must shrug off criticism and get on with the job. If you don't then your critics are winning.

Barry Norman is famed for his straight talking no-nonsense approach to interviews but his presenting style is equally candid. Unlike other television presenters who seem to be cloned from the very same mould, Barry's frank and characteristic on screen manner has earned him cult status among film buffs.

I remember two bits of advice someone once gave me, smile more and don't speak so fast. I ignored them both. What irritates me more than anything is when I see presenters with permanent smiles etched on their faces. They're borrowing it straight from America. You can imagine them still smiling just after they've pronounced World War Three has started. If you're going to be a good presenter you must obey the golden rule, always be yourself. If you pretend to be someone you're not the viewers will know. That's not good.

So what about a little advice if you've just started out on a presenting career yourself? According to Barry the key lies within yourself.

You have got to look comfortable in front of the camera. This sounds easy but it isn't. There are an awful lot of people whose names I won't mention who clearly look uncomfortable on TV.

What I find helps you look more natural is if you look at the centre of the screen when you're reading the autocue. That way it means you don't have to move your eyes. Also, another trick is to read the script in a conversational way. Television is an extension into someone's home so you should chat things to people. Viewers want to be talked to not talked down to.

If your aspirations do lie on the small screen it's worth remembering what Barry Norman has just said. The first thing you're going to have to commit to is hard work. This is standard. Whether you are just starting your career or nearing the end of it, unless you put in all your effort you will never fulfil your ambitions. Corny but true.

Secondly, you must never let criticism hold you back. If it's said in a positive way for you to learn then take note. However, if it's kindled by jealousy you can't allow the comments to engulf you. Dwelling on negativity produces negativity.

Finally, choose a job you love. Barry Norman is fortunate to be working in a field he adores but he didn't just fall into it, he picked it. If you are working in an area of television you truly enjoy you'll want to work harder yourself. Unlike the movies life doesn't provide us with a sequel so as there's only one take it's important to give our best performance. Although we may not become the Robert De Niros of the television world we can certainly be major players. In one of the most competitive industries in the world that in itself deserves an Oscar.

Vanessa Feltz

Value for Money

"If I am not for myself who will be for me? If I am for myself alone what am I and if not now when?"

anessa Feltz has been in the headlines a a great deal in the late 1990s, but rather than good news the publicity surrounding her *Vanessa* show has been less than favourable. With accusations that researchers on the show knowingly allowed fake guests to appear, the BBC decided to pull the plug on it. As the previously undisputed queen of the British talk show Vanessa now has the task of reinventing herself, perhaps in a completely different programme format altogether.

The BBC reputedly paid the star two million pounds for a two-year contract which shows just how highly she's regarded. With this in mind there's no doubt Vanessa will be bouncing back to present another high profile programme. Although the road may not have been smooth for Vanessa recently it's something she's more than used to. Ever since she first broke into broadcasting she's always had to fight her corner.

> When I finished college I didn't really know what I wanted to do. The first career I considered was advertising but those jobs were hardly ever advertised. When I did see ones advertised those I applied for I would often end up getting down to the last three or four and that was it. I wanted to be the person who wrote the jingles but seeing as there was no way I was going to get offered that kind of post I eventually took a post as an editorial assistant on the magazine, *Campaign*. Then after that I went freelance as a journalist. A

189

short time later I was invited onto a Jewish radio programme in London to talk about an article I had written for a magazine. Before I knew it I had my own show and things just took off from there.

Vanessa was asked onto BBC GLR Radio to chat about her article in *The Jewish Chronicle*. Initially she was invited onto the radio show for a one off discussion but impressed the producers so much they offered her a weekly slot for no money. The catch was she wouldn't be paid but within a year she was presenting the show herself. One thing that stood her in good stead then and ever since is total preparation.

I always take everything I do incredibly seriously and have always tried my hardest. When I was asked to do an interview on GLR I spent about four hours working out what I was going to say. I tried to get in as much as possible – funny lines, little gags, everything – it's quite amusing just thinking about it. Having never done any kind of radio before I didn't really know what to expect so I prepared thoroughly. The show itself was only for a minority Jewish audience so probably only had about 200 listeners but to me it was national stuff and millions were listening.

Preparing laboriously became Vanessa's trademark. On her radio show if a guest had written a book she read it. Likewise, if they were an expert in a specific field then she studied it. In later years when Vanessa was interviewing celebrities on *The Big Breakfast* some of them would be amazed just how much she knew about them. But it was another magazine article she wrote which provided Vanessa with her break into television and this time the show she was invited on did have millions of viewers.

I was asked onto *This Morning* with Richard and Judy to talk about a piece I'd penned for *She* magazine. The article was about erogenous zones and it was attracting quite a lot of attention in the press. The discussion went really well and I felt really relaxed. I guess other TV companies thought it went well too because one of them, Anglia, offered me a contract to present the *Vanessa* show. The year was 1994 and it all happened so quickly. We filmed the regional pilots in April and May, the network bought the show in July and then it went out on air in September. I remember the time well because on top of all this my family and I were moving house!

Vanessa had married a junior hospital doctor when she was 22 and since then two children had arrived. To say her daily schedule was hectic was an understatement. But, despite having to juggle several things around at once, the *Vanessa* show was an instant success and the presenter soon established herself as a rising star. Fame followed quickly and although the recognition was nice to begin with the novelty soon began to wear off.

I always tell aspiring presenters that I would think very hard about whether or not fame is something they really want because by the time you've got it it's too late. Once you're famous that's it, you can't 'un-fame' yourself. Before you start getting recognised fame is not something you really think about because you never really feel it's going to happen to you. The difficult part to cope with is the invasion of your privacy, it's sometimes unbelievable. My sister's been door-stepped twice about me and she's a teacher who's got nothing to do with anything. Then there was the summer before last when we were on holiday abroad. Reporters were chasing us around trying to find out why I'd finished at Anglia Television and how much the BBC had offered me! Of course there are huge compensations for working in television like the money and a varied lifestyle but believe me the fame thing can be trying. The highs are high but the lows can be very low.

One thing Vanessa is well known for is her ability to reach out to the viewer at home. People respect her because they can relate to her. In a medium that takes no prisoners this is not an easy task to accomplish. The other skill Vanessa has mastered is being able to think on her feet. In live television this is one thing that is essential as the talk show hostess herself can testify.

I can think of quite a number of occasions when I have had to think pretty sharpish but a memorable time was when I was working on *The Big Breakfast*. Each morning I used to interview a different celebrity on the bed and there was this one instance when the camera switched live to me two minutes before it should have done. I think I was still doing my hair at the time! Two minutes may not sound a lot but in television terms it's quite a length. What happened was we were filming a guy attempting to abseil down the side of the studios and one of our cameramen had decided to abseil next to him to get a better shot. This was good in theory but not in practice because just as the cameraman and the abseiler were nearing the bottom they suddenly gained speed and there was this almighty crash. After that complete darkness. No-one knew what had happened and whether the cameraman had died or anything so the producer decided to cut to me! 'Fill fill fill' he shouted! The difficult part was to know what to say and how to say it. I didn't want to sound too chirpy in case the poor chap had died but at the same time I didn't want to sound too depressing. Somehow I managed to fill.

Despite a few bruises, particularly to his pride, the cameraman survived – but so too had Vanessa. Holding the fort for two minutes without any aid is quite a task. Throughout the years Vanessa has learned to cope with similar situations, especially on her talk shows. Let's face it, if anything's going to happen then it's usually on this kind of programme. But despite her success the greatest achievement in Vanessa's eyes is actually breaking into television in the first place.

I think I encountered almost every single obstacle there is to encounter in television. For a start there is no set structure in the industry and that can be terribly intimidating when you're first starting out. I often ended up asking myself just how I was expected to break in? I know for journalists there's the BBC training scheme but to me that was almost impossible to get onto because so many people were going for it. Then I'd hear stories like how the current head of BBC daytime TV started out as a secretary 22 years ago then worked her way up. When you've got a degree should you really have to start at that level as a secretary? These were the sorts of thoughts going around my mind and if you're trying to get your first break it can be very confusing. I think if your mother's a TV producer or your father's a journalist then they can tell you which way to go about things but for majority of us without connections it's difficult.

The key is to stick at it just like Vanessa did. Persistence can bore through even the hardiest of obstacles. Just look at Vanessa – starting out without any knowledge about radio, let alone television, she has still managed to make it. If that's not inspiring then little else is.

A journalistic background is a great way of getting into the entertainment industry, it's a solid base. I've noticed that some people snipe at you if they think you haven't had proper journalistic training. If you can turn round to those kind of people and say, 'I started off at the *Swindon Evening Echo*' or whatever then that's always going to work in your favour because people will assume that you actually have some idea of what you're doing. If you haven't got that kind of background then you're going to have to work doubly hard to prove you're good. I'm not saying you need a journalistic background but I think it certainly helps.

Jumping straight into television is difficult. With no experience to provide momentum you can often end up falling flat on your face. A good way is to step into TV via newspapers or radio. These stepping stones are the tried and tested route in.

Local radio is a great place to begin because a lot of television companies recruit from this area. Naturally it's something that's a lot easier to get into as well if you can help out on an evening show or something. It doesn't matter whether you start off answering the phone for no pay the important thing is at least your face will become familiar. I didn't get paid anything for a year on the show I first appeared on. The more your face gets known the more chance you have of getting promoted internally because that's where the jobs come from. You're not going to get anywhere from the outside unless people know your face on the inside. It's how it works.

For a jobbing journalist who first started writing articles on hair care Vanessa Feltz has proved her worth. Despite facing the task of shaking off criticism that led to the demise of the Vanessa show she's proved she's got what it takes to fight back. As well as her consumer programme *Value For Money* which is in its fourth year she has more peak-time programmes in the pipeline. Knowing how hard it can be to make it in the business and to stay there once you've arrived has left her sympathetic to those just starting out themselves.

I've been there so I know what it's like. The good news is it's not impossible and doing it the hard way makes success even sweeter. My advice is don't worry about things but instead get out there and do it. Without action you're not going to get anywhere. Go out and get your face seen because if no one's seeing your face or your work then you're not getting anywhere. Get used to the idea that when you first start you'll be working for nothing. I doubt you'll meet many other TV broadcasters who didn't.

John Stapleton

GMTV

"A television presenter is like a professional footballer. You've got a limited time on the pitch, you can suddenly be dropped for no reason and you're always prone to mishaps."

*P*anorama, *Nationwide, Newsnight, Watchdog, The Time The Place.* You would think with these credits to his name and 29 years in the business John Stapleton would now be relaxing and enjoying life a little. Apparently not.

> No way. You just can't afford to get complacent. I'd love to say I was less intimidated by television but the truth is I'm not. For a start the technology is changing all the while, so you're constantly having to keep up with that. Then there are all the bright young people now entering the business keeping me on my toes. Sometimes I really do feel like a dinosaur.

This particular presenter seems good at evading extinction and in this industry that's no mean feat. While countless other presenters have followed the plight of the T-Rex, never to be seen again, John Stapleton is still roaming the TV world. Right now he's co-presenting the news hour on GMTV. With five million early risers tuning in to watch each day week John's proving he still has box office appeal.

I must admit I'm a lucky guy. I've travelled all around the world at the BBC's expense and I'm still working on a top programme. That aspect of the job is brilliant and is one of the good things about television. But journalism can be a wretched business too – especially if you're a presenter. It's a very subjective job. One minute you can be flavour of the month and next you can be out on your ear. When that happens there's no point trying to rationalise it and no point questioning yourself. More often than not it's simply because the powers that be prefer someone else. It's the nature of the business and you just have to live with it.

John Stapleton has had to live with it a few times. There was the time he was suddenly axed from TVam and then the occasion *The Time, The Place* was suddenly taken off air. But most damning in John's mind was when he was fired from the BBC's *Breakfast Time*.

It was awful. On the day it happened Tony Hall, the Head of News, called me into his office. Ten minutes later I stepped out of it without a job. It was totally unexpected. There wasn't even a yellow card never mind the red one. I remember coming out of Television Centre and walking down Wood Lane towards Lime Grove. It was the longest bloody walk I've ever made. I felt desolate, absolutely desolate, and it took me six months to get over it. I thought it was a real kick in the teeth. The worst part was there was no real explanation. The only thing Tony said was they wanted a change. As it turned out Nicholas Witchell took over my post. People tell you not to take it personally but it's very personal. That kind of news is very hard to take.

It was at the tender age of 13 that John first knew he wanted to be a journalist. As soon as he turned 16 he began writing off to newspapers for jobs. Very few replied so one day John decided to follow up his letters with a visit.

I had an aunt who lived in London and one weekend while I was staying with her I decided to call on the *Hornsey Journal* in Tottenham. I'd written to the News Editor a few weeks earlier but had got no response. When I turned up I asked the receptionist if I could see him. She looked at me coaxingly through her glasses for a second and buzzed him. When he came out I asked him why he hadn't replied to my letter. 'How old are you?' he asked. 'Fifteen' I replied. After pausing a second and wiping a wry smile from his face he finally inquired, 'Does your mother know you're here?!'

It's this kind of relentless determination which has powered John Stapleton to the top. Even before he reached his teens he was already displaying all the ingredients needed to make a successful journalist. Persistence especially. When he was 16 he even applied for a senior reporter position with BBC Radio Manchester – this with no experience. It just goes to show if you think big you can achieve big. Although you may not get what you want at the time a positive attitude eventually reaps rewards.

John first started his career in his home town of Oldham. After working for the *Oldham Evening Chronicle* he moved on to the *Daily Sketch* in Manchester then to the *Daily Sketch* in London. His first break in television came as a researcher for *This Is Your Life*. Slowly moving upwards he moved to the *Today* show and was soon writing links for one of the most infamous presenters of the day, Bill Grundy. It was time to learn what television was all about.

> You're bound to get knockbacks whatever career you first start off in, but I remember the first setback I had left a lasting impression on me. It was from Bill Grundy at Thames Television who in those days was a real hero of mine. At the time I was writing for his show but he knew that what I really wanted to be was a reporter. One day when we were talking in the corridor he told me he thought I would never make it. He just came straight out with it. I remember being devastated because he was such an icon. But not long afterwards I did get promoted to reporter and the day I got the new job Bill came up to me and said he was wrong. I'll never forget that moment because it just shows the measure of the man.

When someone questions your ability it's very easy to allow your confidence to drain away but there's no time to wallow in self-pity. On the contrary, it's time to work even harder. Somebody has just set down a challenge and it is up to you to overcome it. Sometimes we all need a little leverage in life to push us forward and people who raise concern about our talents can often provide this. You'll find most people in this book have similar stories to tell but rather than dwell on their faults they have addressed them. This kind of action is what separates them from the rest.

I think it's encounters of this kind which sorts the wheat from the chaff. In TV journalism only the strong survive – the others get out while they can. In the beginning you've got to be honest with yourself – you've got to ask whether you're capable of taking the knocks. If the answer is no then you won't like television and if you don't like television then by God it will show.

Most people, I'm sure, know what they're going into when they decide to follow a career in journalism but it's comforting to know no one else gets an easy ride. Far from it. Even when you've finally managed to break in and made it past the first few years there are still obstacles to overcome. As a presenter it's managing to keep afloat after you've been pushed head first into the water.

My first major test came when I was asked to host the Miss United Kingdom contest. At the time people laughed and smiled but it was actually one of the scariest times of my life. I didn't even have an autocue. I had to totally ad-lib. The show lasted 50 minutes but it seemed more like 10 hours. There were 33 girls stepping on and off the stage and the only time I was allowed to look at my prompt card was when I was reading out their essentials. Terrifying! The worst part was I only got paid £75. But good did come out of it because I went back to present *Nationwide* the following week and I remember thinking, 'God this is a doddle. If I can present a Miss United Kingdom contest without so much as an autocue then I can do anything.'

During his career John found another problem was getting work at the BBC. In the seventies, especially, he felt the corporation was particularly prone to elitism.

> I think a lot of people who worked back then will admit that if you didn't have a degree from a University like Oxford or Cambridge, then you could forget the BBC. The old boy network was at its peak. As a working class lad myself who wasn't very well educated at all it was tough to get work there. I think the network still exists today and although it's not nearly so bad it's still hard to crack. Don't get me wrong, I have a lot of friends who work at the BBC but when you apply for a job there you will sometimes be faced with the question, 'Are you one of us?'

John Stapleton is proud of his roots. His father worked as a secretary at the local Co-op store and his mother was an unqualified school teacher. Describing himself as a working class lad who's done alright John says his secret of success is down to enjoying his work. If you like your work then you put more effort in. If you put more effort in then you'll reap more rewards. This simple philosophy has served him well.

> When I first entered television I gave myself 10 years. Twenty-nine years on I'm still here and I don't take that for granted. I've never considered myself to be a megastar but I think I've always been in and around the premiership division. I'm not an international but I'm a good club player. There's no shame in that and I'm delighted to have been given the opportunity.

When you speak with John Stapleton there's no bitterness in his voice at all – just a hint of satisfaction that he's managed to play the system and stay on top of it. He knows about the pressures young people in the business are faced with these days and he's only too happy to give out advice.

> I think if you've decided to go for it then you've got to make sure you give everything 150 per cent. You've got to

understand that it's not going to be easy but then again what job is these days? There will be times during your career when you will be humiliated and when your confidence is shattered. You must get over this and remember most other people experience this too. You've got to learn to live with it. There will also be times when people appear not to love you and this can be hard. Presenters are like little dogs who need to be stroked, pampered and reassured. We are only people after all and you need to be told that what you're doing is OK.

You will also meet bullies in this industry, I mean there's no argument about it, this business creates monsters. Having said that though when you do hit a low just remind yourself why you entered television. It's a tremendous thing to be involved in and nothing gives you a greater buzz than live TV. It's a great feeling knowing you're the first person to pass on news to someone else. I'm actually a terrible gossip but I think you have to be to become a good journalist.

In his mid-fifties John Stapleton is a seasoned pro and for the most part knows what it takes to be a major player. To hit a home run in this game strength and determination are not the only things you need. Thick skin is also required to protect you from the ball of criticism that can sometimes be hurled at you. This can lead to self-doubt and if that takes hold it's sometimes hard to shake off.

At the same time you must ensure your own bases are covered. If you don't someone may steal in behind you. Only by acknowledging then strengthening your weaknesses can prevent this from happening. Being a television journalist or presenter is one of the most privileged professions in the world but you've got to earn your position. As John Stapleton can testify the road to success isn't always easy but when you finally get there the rewards are worth it.

Philippa Forrester

Photo: Nicky Johnson

Tomorrow's World

"Before you try for a career in television my advice is check yourself out first. Your love of the job has got to be genuine if you expect to do well in it."

If the definition of a top TV presenter is someone who's able to turn their hand to anything then Philippa Forrester is a prime candidate. Starting her career in children's television before venturing into the scientific realms of *Tomorrow's World* and *Robot Wars* she also presents the pet programme *Barking Mad* and transport series *Dream Machine*. Not surprisingly, her work schedule is hectic and a seven day week all too common.

> If people knew how hard television can be I think lots would be genuinely shocked. It's not just about appearing in front of the screen, there's an awful lot of preparation involved too. Some people just don't grasp that. Of course it can also be great fun too but this is usually proceeded by lots of hard work.

Like others before her, Philippa is a firm believer in doing something for the right reasons. Forget the glamour and forget the money, if you want to work in television then passion should ride high on your list.

> The first thing I always say is check yourself out. Ask yourself a few questions. Is your interest in TV genuine? Do you really know what it involves? Have you been to a studio to see how a programme goes out? Does it excite you? Are you prepared to stand outside in the freezing cold for hours

on end just to get one shot? If you're in it for the right reasons then you will have answered yes to all these questions. You've got to know what something entails before you go for it.

Philippa's fascination with television first began in the historic Hampshire town of Winchester where she grew up. One particular day the recreation centre burnt down and a huge crowd gathered to watch the spectacle. Rather than watching the firefighters battling with flames, Philippa was more captivated with a local TV crew which had turned up to film the event. The way the team operated was just entrancing.

> I have always loved television. In the beginning I didn't know what I wanted to do – producing or directing – but I knew right away that TV was the place for me. There's just something incredible about working in it and it has got to be one of the most fascinating professions in the world.

Winchester Hospital Radio was where Philippa first got involved with broadcasting and it provided her with the perfect introduction. While she was there she got in touch with a journalist working in regional TV news in Southampton who invited her into the station to see how things worked. Sitting in on edits and watching how the reporter interviewed people convinced Philippa that she too wanted to go for journalism.

When she turned 18 Philippa travelled to Birmingham where she studied a three year course in English at the city's university. The college boasted its very own TV station and offered students the chance to try everything from engineering to presenting.

> We would get together every lunchtime and produce absolutely anything from puppet shows and greyhound racing to mini James Bond films. It was fantastic experience. I remember a guy from BBC Pebble Mill came in to give us a talk. He told us to make sure we made the most of our time there because if we did enter TV afterwards then we'd always be making programmes the way other people wanted.

As well as being great fun we also discovered what television was all about. I learned about edit suites, how to shoot pictures and how to fill time as a presenter. It was an ideal training ground.

For many people, giving up their lunch break or spare time to work at something is a major sacrifice. When you're a student, especially, cheap drinks at the bar and an array of parties on offer are too tempting by far. But for Philippa it was never a problem. The TV work she did as a student was what she loved more than anything and there was nothing she would rather have worked on. The same can be said for the rest of her career.

When you love doing something then you shouldn't see the work you put in as a big sacrifice. When I was younger and working at a hospital radio station in my spare time it didn't bother me at all that the other children were going off to parties. I adored what I was doing. That's the key to working in television – it should never feel like you're making any sacrifices at all. If it does then it means your heart isn't in the job.

Philippa's major TV break came when she was invited down to London to watch the BBC children's TV show *Going Live!* From the comfort of the gallery Philippa saw how the programme was made and she got chatting to the floor manager who explained how everything worked. Shortly afterwards one of the show's presenters, Philip Schofield, walked into the gallery and he too talked her through the programme.

Philip in particular was wonderful because he gave me so much of his time. Before our meeting I had always considered becoming a journalist but after I got talking to him I realised that presenting was a fascinating job too. I loved the performance involved and the communication. As well as telling me about the benefits of presenting Philip also told me the downsides to the job. When you're live on air and everything goes wrong you're the one who has to take the flak. That kind of pressure can be daunting.

Impressed with Philippa's obvious enthusiasm Philip told her to speak to the deputy editor in the presentation department for more advice. What he didn't reveal was that the BBC was actually looking for a presenter. Expecting a five minute chat, Philippa spent an hour and a half talking about herself and her ambitions. A week later she received a letter at home inviting her for an audition.

> I thought it was very strange because they knew I was still at university. Still, seven days later I caught the train down to London and a couple of things actually worked in my favour. The first was that because I thought they weren't looking for a presenter at that particular time I didn't put any unnecessary pressure on myself. My nerves weren't really a problem. Secondly, the night before the audition I had a premonition that I'd got the job. I dreamed that as I was nervously walking along the corridors of Television Centre people were coming up to me telling me not to worry because I had got it. It's a strange tale but true!

What also helped at the audition was Philippa's experience at the student TV station. When the producers told her to fill for 60 seconds she knew they meant a minute and not a second more or less. When she finally started her new job it was as a BBC children's presenter in *The Broom Cupboard*. The cupboard was the small studio where the presenter read the links.

You've probably learned by now that even though television offers the high life there are also times when an area of depression is not far away. Philippa encountered a low-ebb a year after she had landed the broom cupboard job. At the time she was presenting it on a part-time basis while she was still at university but assumed she would get it full-time once she had finished.

> Unfortunately, the BBC decided to give the job to a young presenter called Toby Anstis because they felt it was better to have a boy fronting the programme. That was hard for me and I was suddenly confronted by all kinds of negative questions. Was it because I wasn't good enough? Did this mean it was the end of my career? Where would I go next? It

was terrible because I honestly thought there was nowhere else to go with Children's BBC afterwards. It was a real time of self-doubt and the whole experience really knocked me for six.

Like many experiences in life, although it felt like the end of the world things eventually worked out for Philippa. Rather than being defeatist and just giving up the new presenter sought work elsewhere. Soon the Disney Channel had hired her and she presented on GMTV. Looking back she's a stronger and wiser person.

> I have this philosophy that you can beat your head against a rock for as long as you like but it's never going to move. The only way you are ever going to get around it is by changing direction. When you do that and you're eventually around it you'll often find that the new direction you took was actually a lot better than the one you were first going for. If that route hadn't been blocked then you would never have discovered the new better one. Sometimes we all need a few rocks to make us change course and although we don't always see it at the time things often work out more in our favour. Take my career. If I had got the *Broom Cupboard* job on BBC1 then I probably wouldn't be doing what I am now - that is presenting a variety of programmes that I adore. In hindsight I've got a lot to thank for that rock I encountered back then.

Wise words. When you ask Philippa to reflect on her career she immediately takes you back to an experience she had at a drinks party last year. Philippa was invited to the party by the Controller of BBC Television, Peter Salmon. He'd organised the gathering to celebrate the BBC's science department which had enjoyed a successful year. Its *Twister Week* and *Eclipse Special* had been particularly triumphant with the latter programme attracting a massive 13 million viewers.

> While I was at the party I managed to slip away for half an hour to reflect on the last few years of my life. It was being

held on the sixth floor where CBBC used to be situated and I just couldn't resist nipping out for another look at the place. As I stood in the corridor I tried to think back to what it felt like before I'd managed to make a real go of my career. What struck me as the toughest challenges to deal with back then were things totally of my own making, my own insecurities about myself – was I any good at the job? what would happen if I wasn't? – those kinds of questions. Also, I remember being very very tired back then because I was working six days a week and I was suddenly on my own living in London. These were the hardest things to get over and as I stood in the same dark corridors with no one else around it was very weird reflecting on them all again. Looking back I think I had the same doubts everyone else does in that position. The fact I have progressed since proves that they can be beaten.

Inspired by what you've just read? If you're ready to embark on a career in television then just remember it won't all be plain sailing.

Drive and being in the job because you love it is vital. When you're in something like television you should never want to let it go. It's also partly luck whether you succeed, not just in terms of opportunity, but who you are surrounded by. If you've got enough people who support you through the rough times and who criticise you so that you learn then that's good. No-one starts off brilliantly – just remember that. When you're thrown into a high profile job you're bound to make mistakes. When I started I was absolutely awful but if you can learn quickly then you'll be ok. I often have glimpses where I think I love this job very much. Television is one of the few professions which can provide a feeling like that.

The Future: Multimedia & Digital

7

The Future: Multimedia & Digital

The Internet

The effect the Internet is having on broadcasting is phenomenal. For years the main channels access into our lives for electronically distributed information have been radio and TV, but that is now changing. People are discovering that the Net is an excellent source for obtaining information quickly.

One role that's being redefined is modern day journalism. Many people claim they no longer read newspapers because the same information can be collected from the Net. There is significant criticism that the current print media don't allow for a dynamic response or follow up articles in hand.

After major incidents the Internet is becoming the popular medium of choice for users. Rather than tuning to a news channel, people curious to find out about a new story turn to the Net for information. Big events are often reported and discussed live on *Internet Relay Chats*.

The advantage the Internet has over television, radio and newspapers is users are in control. With the Net they can receive information whenever and can comment about it as it happens. Usenet newsgroups and mailing lists provide a media where people can articulate their understandings. Having the ability to control the mass media like this is becoming popular. People know the news can't get any newer because they're receiving it as it breaks. Martyn Moore, the editor of the magazine *Internet* says over the next five years the relationship between broadcasting and the Net will see a fantastic growth.

> At the minute technology is limiting what can actually happen between the TV and the Internet. That will soon change. In the not too distant future what we will see is a much more interactive service between the two. Television and the Internet will combine to form a medium where the user is in total control. Remote control pads will be replaced by more sophisticated keyboards which offer the viewer wider choices. In a way the technology will develop from what Sky is already offering with its interactive sports service. Viewers will control what they see on screen and access information about what they see at the touch of a button. They will also be able to communicate with other people about what they're watching as it happens. It's very exciting.

Companies like Microsoft and AT & T are also predicting that within five years the television set in the corner of our living rooms will provide a very different function to the one it provides today. It will cease to be just a 'TV' and instead become our 'Multimedia Console'. This multi-functional apparatus will offer satellite and cable programmes, digital terrestrial output, videophone connectivity and the Internet.

The immediacy of the Internet is one advantage television has over print journalism and is something every channel is now exploiting. TV chiefs know that to compete with the Net broadcasting has to change. This metamorphosis is already happening and involves a closer relationship with the Internet. Every major news channel now has a web site. If you click online with the BBC you can actually download audio clips of the days bulletins and its pages are regularly refreshed. Sky News is also committed to its Internet news service. It has launched an interactive news programme where users can communicate directly with a newscaster live on television. Talking about various issues they can register their vote about topics of the day.

This technology of change represents a fundamental challenge to the way that news is broadcast. Online discussion groups allow open and free discourse and this is something people will regard as standard in the future. If you watch current affairs programmes or chat shows on TV you will know that many invite responses from viewers via e-mail. Internet communication like this will expand and soon most programmes will allow this kind of engagement.

It's not just national stations that are changing; regional channels are also investing heavily in the future. Every local station now has a web page as the Web Development Manager for United Broadcasting & Entertainment, Robyn Oneile, can testify.

> The global trend in broadcasting, particularly at regional stations, is towards news and current affairs. Because of the exponential growth of the World Wide Web, and the immediacy of its information delivery, radio and television broadcasters are being forced to embrace this new technology and find ways of working with it. Broadcasters realise that programmes aired on screen also need to be broadcast on the Net. They know that the Internet can complement what is broadcast on TV by providing more detailed information on its pages. The way things are headed, newcomers to broadcasting need to be well versed in the new technologies that will form our multimedia future. Producers and presenters will not only find themselves making programmes for TV but also for the Internet. Internet time moves four times faster than real time so the multimedia era is about to dawn.

Digital Television

Digital television is a new, more efficient method of broadcasting which allows for greater choice. Digital transmission can fit several channels into the space currently used to transmit just one analogue channel. In time, all households are likely to view programmes that are digitally transmitted when the analogue transmitters are eventually turned off for good.

The advantage for viewers is that this digital technology (terrestrial, satellite and cable) can create around 200 new channels. It also offers services like wide screen picture and improved sound quality. Interactive services like home banking, shopping and Internet access are also being made available.

Digital television can be received in three ways; through a satellite dish, through a cable connection and via an existing television aerial. Viewers can choose any of these but need to buy or rent a set top box decoder. This device reassembles the pictures. Soon most television sets will have built-in decoders.

Although analogue transmissions will continue for some time pressure is being put on the government to switch them off. Television companies and manufacturers have invested heavily in the digital revolution and at the minute viewers are remaining apathetic. Poor sales mean poor returns and this is bad news for companies. Many people connected to satellite or cable believe they already have enough channels and are not interested in receiving more. There is also a reluctance to invest in something that is still developing. The government is considering switching off the analogue transmitters in 2010 but this could be brought forward. If digital sales don't improve the government may be forced to shut down transmitters earlier to avoid digital companies losing a fortune.

Interactive TV

If you're an avid football fan you'll already know that Sky was the first company to launch interactive TV. The interactive programming is the first of its kind anywhere in the world and offers viewers a new way of watching sport. Available on Sky's digital sports channel its live interactive football matches provides a number of options at the mere touch of a button.

Firstly, the match can be seen from a different position enabling the viewer to choose the view of the game. Secondly, at any point in the match viewers can watch key moments such as goals, saves and free kicks. Statistics are also available offering information on the match, its players and league table details. Finally, if you want to see any part of the action again all you have to do is hit the replay button.

This new kind of system is revolutionary and has enormous ramifications for every other genre of programming. Interactive sports matches could soon be joined by news programmes and even movies. The pioneering system is being watched closely by other stations, particularly in America, where the same programme is being launched there.

Although still in its infancy, interactive TV looks set to expand. In the not too distant future the system will be able to offer the viewer even more control of what they see on screen. As digital television takes off it's wise to try and keep abreast of such technology and what it means for broadcasting as a whole. Just remember, if you want to work in the industry then you'll be a part of that future too.

Restricted Services Licences

Although they're not connected to the digital network it's worth mentioning 'Restricted Services Licences.' RSLs are a form of broadcasting that could be the springboard you're looking for into terrestrial TV. Like restrictive service radio licences RSLs are powered by small transmitters meaning broadcasting is confined to limited areas.

RSLs are awarded by the ITC (Independent Television Commission) on a leasehold basis and they usually last for two years. Several cities in the United Kingdom have already started broadcasting on these special licences including the Isle of Wight and Oxford. Many others plan to follow their lead and it's estimated that within a few years most major towns and cities will be broadcasting on an RSL channel.

This type of TV is already hugely popular in the United States with many stations broadcasting 24-hours. For people interested in the medium but with no real experience they're an ideal place to learn what television is all about. Just like local television newsrooms RSL stations employ video journalists, directors and technical operators.

Most places have a studio where live debates are aired and programmes hosted by a presenter.

Because they are run on tight budgets these kinds of stations usually employ people on little or no wages. If you're prepared to offer your time and skills for free then the chances of gaining work at one are high. Getting some kind of experience in broadcasting is essential if you want to make a career in television and an RSL station can provide the perfect introduction.

One of the latest cities in the United Kingdom to start broadcasting on an RSL is Bristol. Unlike most other stations which broadcast live from a studio, 'City TV' doesn't contain any live television at all. All the programming is pre-recorded with video journalists shooting half-hour length features on 'topical topics.' 'City TV's' Project Manager, Adrian Brenard, says the training it offers is unique.

> When you look at the facts there aren't that many opportunities for people to get involved with local telly. That is until now. RSL stations mean people now have the chance to work in a medium which, for years, has previously been out of reach. Just like with local newspapers people are able to have their say in what goes out in their community. That's important. On the other side of the spectrum people who are interested in television as a career are able to use it as a platform for greater things. Everyone who works at the station is learning off each other all the time and it's a superb training ground.

So, if you haven't already, why not check out whether your town is getting ready to launch its own channel? Although technically there are a few places where RSL's can't be broadcast there's bound to be a neighbouring town or city that is broadcasting locally. If not, there should be very shortly.

Famous last words...

8

Famous last words...

If you're not totally brilliant then you're going to have to get up earlier, work harder and run faster than the rest. The only place where success comes before work is in the dictionary.

Graham Miller, **ITN Sport**

Never let anyone tell you that you can't do it. I was told to stick to radio when I was 24 and that television wasn't for me.

Michael Buerk, **BBC News**

I am a very strong believer in things happening for a reason. If you want something badly enough then you can make it happen, it doesn't matter what it is. I think I've got one of the best jobs in the world. You can get one too if you put your mind to it.

Zoë Ball, **Radio 1**

Television presenters and reporters are merely the face and voice of a vast team of professionals. If you mess up you're messing up the work of your colleagues. If that's not embarrassing enough a couple of million people are watching as well.

Ray Stubbs, **BBC Sport**

A diamond is only a piece of coal that stuck with it.

Anne Davies, **GMTV**

What bothers me these days is people seem to be going into broadcasting because it seems an agreeable life. Let me tell you it's not. When I first started I spent a lot of time standing around on cold wet corners of Belfast, a lot of time going to wars and a lot of time swimming through treacle. Even now I find myself swimming through treacle and there are days when my job is profoundly unsatisfying.

Jeremy Paxman, **Newsnight**

Those who can do. Those who can't talk about it!

Murray Walker, **ITV Motor Racing**

As journalists we must learn to report and analyse success and achievement just as much as failure. We should not be vultures swooping down from some remote mountain top eyrie to feed on the carcasses of the teeming masses below. We are part of that society shaping its attitudes and its future. This means we have responsibilities to it.

Martyn Lewis, **BBC News**

Always keep a notepad you can fit in your pocket!

David Foster, **Sky Business News**

There's no such thing as a shortcut to hard work in television. If you want to make it to the top in broadcasting you've got to be master of your own universe. This means complete focus and absolute commitment.

Gabby Yorath, **ITV Sport**

Never give up what you dream for because persistence and determination will always get you there.

Stephen Mulhern, **Children's ITV**

You can never rush a snail.

Nick Baker, **Tomorrow's World**

It's easy to forget what impression television has on the great British public. Invading someone's living room everyday is a privilege that should never be abused. Be honest.

Kay Burley, **Sky News**

Television journalists should never underestimate the importance of cameramen and tape editors. Good ones will always make you look better than you actually do and very good ones can help you sound more intelligent than you are.

Tom Skippings, **Sky Sport**

The world is full of people who want to be on telly. But there's only one quarter-Chinese, northern, gangly, law graduate with a daft name and a keen interest in consumer affairs. Build on what you alone can offer – and you never have real competition.

***Chris Choi*, ITN**

Conclusion

9

Conclusion

Someone once told me that wherever you go you'll never see a shy millionaire. The reason is because to make a million you've got to put yourself about. The same applies to successful people in the media. To get to the top in this industry you've got to continually push yourself forward. At the end of the day obstacles are par for the course in anyone's life, the sooner we accept that, the sooner we can start focusing on how to beat them.

After reading the interviews in this book I hope you're now convinced that few people make it far by luck alone. Contrary to popular belief, in this profession there is no such thing as an easy ride and even if you do chance upon fame through a lucky break, if you're no good then you'll soon be found out. What's the point in waiting for an opportunity to arise if you can't back it up with ability?

Now we've read about the kinds of problems that lie ahead we should be armed with more confidence, after all, if we already know our enemy before commencing battle then our chances of winning are higher. During our quest, for example, we know that enemy number one will be competition. In one of the toughest industries in the world to break into, competition is rife, but why should that worry us? We've learned now that if we focus on our own skills rather than worrying about other peoples then we stand more chance at excelling.

Enemy number two is making sacrifices. Unfortunately, this particular encounter is unavoidable. Whether it's the long hours or missing important social events because of work we have to accept them. Not everyone does of course – and that is the difference between those at the top of the ladder and those stuck at the bottom.

The third enemy, and perhaps the most dangerous, is self-doubt. Never underestimate it. All it takes is one little knockback to sow the seed and if we let it take hold the results can prove disastrous. As a presenter the problem may be questioning our talent. I'm sure this is a common fear among many presenters just starting out and the only antidote is experience. As a reporter we may question our writing or interviewing skills. The only cure here is practice. As a producer we may doubt our own decisions. Whatever may cause self-doubt to surface it's vital to stamp it out right away. Lack of confidence does not inspire people and does not produce results.

My experience in writing *Broadcasting: Breaking Down the Barriers* really has convinced me that 'if you believe you will achieve.' There's no doubt about it! I can use this book as an example. When I first thought about writing it my immediate response was negative. Firstly, I told myself I had no chance of getting the interviews. Why would anyone high up in the business want to speak to me? Secondly, I decided there was no way I would be able to find the time. My evenings and weekends were very important to me and not up for discussion. Looking back it seems quite amazing. In less than the time it had taken me to think of the idea I had already convinced myself not to pursue it. Then I started thinking and I cast my mind back to the many other occasions I had used these sorts of excuses for not doing something. There were lots of instances. Appalled by the sheer number I immediately set myself a goal, to finish the challenge that I actually set myself. Up until then this was something I had never really achieved.

The first obstacle I encountered was getting the interviews. This was difficult. Excuses from people were varied, and at times imaginative, but usually that they were too busy to find the time. After a steady stream of rejections had flowed through my letterbox

I decided a different approach was required. So far it had seemed a good idea to explain to people what my book was about in a letter. This clearly wasn't working. Similarly, talking to people through their agents was bearing no fruit either. I decided what I needed was a fresh approach, I needed to meet them face to face. This way at least it would be harder for them to say no.

One classic example is when I tried to get hold of Trevor McDonald. As you can probably imagine Trevor is a very busy man and when he's not reading the news then he's usually working on other projects. I guessed, therefore, that writing a letter would most likely be useless. As one of the biggest names in television he must get hundreds of requests. With this in mind I figured the most effective tactic would be to hang around the ITN studios and literally go up to him. They say the direct approach is often the best so it was time to put the theory to the test.

After choosing my day (and plucking up the courage) I sat myself in the corner of the reception area and waited. I'd been told Trevor usually arrived for work early in the afternoon so it was just a question of being patient. Eventually it paid off and after about an hour I finally spotted him entering the studios. Before he'd had a chance to pass me I was on him like a flash and, spluttering out my request for an interview, I was more than a little surprised when he nodded his head and agreed. Walking off he told me to phone his PA the next day. Thinking I'd managed to secure one of the biggest names in news with relative ease I must admit I was somewhat pleased with myself. I might have known then that this would be short lived!

As promised, the following day I phoned his PA and getting out our diaries we started to work out a date. It soon became apparent though that Trevor was booked solidly on other projects for the next two months, and that included a holiday. The conversation finished with a request for me to phone back in eight weeks time. Naturally, I was disappointed but nevertheless when two months were up I phoned again. The problem was this time the PA herself was on holiday and trying to get a message to

Trevor through the temporary secretary covering her proved impossible. After about eight phone calls I decided to call it a day and implement plan B.

Plan B involved meeting Trevor face to face again, but this time more subtly as if by accident! To make it work I needed to get into Gray's Inn Road one evening. Fortunately, an old friend of mine was working there as a freelance so he was able to sign me in as a guest. Once inside I headed straight for the ground floor canteen, pinning my hopes on the fact that Trevor would grab coffee at some point that night.

As it happens the wait wasn't long and after just 20 minutes I spotted him get into the glass elevator and descend towards the ground floor. Knowing this was my chance I jumped from my seat and raced to the drinks machine. Grabbing a mug I poured a cup of coffee as slowly as I possibly could and waited until Trevor was right behind me before I finished pouring and turned around. It was timed to perfection and in a way I feel sorry for Trevor because there was just no escaping me! Just two minutes after the 'fancy bumping into you' line I'd managed to secure the interview. Luckily for me he remembered our first encounter and after I'd explained how I couldn't get any messages to him since he promised to organise a date with his PA the very next day. The rest as they say is history.

The morale of this story is very simple – never give up! It doesn't matter what the scenario, if you apply enough perseverance to anything in life then you're going to get results - and that includes getting the job you want in broadcasting. Just remember that everyone who works in television, no matter who they are, will have all had to persevere at some point to get to where they are today. If they've had to do it then so will we. Similarly, if they can succeed we can too.

Getting back to the book, another problem I faced when writing it was actually finding the time. As I had just moved to London to pursue a freelance career my main priority was finding work. Most of my day was spent sending off applications and meeting news editors. On top of this I was working different shift patterns. The only way around this problem was to make sacrifices – there was just no way round it. Working weekends and late nights therefore became familiar territory.

The final obstacle barring my way was lack of confidence. Would this book really be good enough to get published or was I just wasting my time? What if I was putting a whole lot of effort into something that in the end might just finish up in the bin? The way I defeated this negativity was by thinking back to the people I had interviewed. I remembered some of them had been dogged by self-doubt in the beginning too. The way they had got over it was by asking themselves one simple question; what's the point of doing anything in life if you don't think it's going to work? The answer is even simpler – there is no point therefore you just have to believe. As I carried on writing the book and the interviews began building up I eventually began to feel more confident with the product. Rather than dwelling on failure I decided that if a publisher didn't like the finished material I would chop it and change it until I eventually found one who did. Positive thinking!

Although there's a lot to be said for positive thinking, there's also a lot to be said for self-belief. To really make an impression in television you're going to need both. If like me you sometimes question your faith in yourself when nothing seems to be working out it's comforting to know every person featured in this book has experienced the same. It seems to be standard. Success doesn't come easy and before we get to taste it we'll usually have to sample a good measure of rejection first. It maybe hard to accept sometimes but, unfortunately, it appears to be par for the course.

Going into television for all the right reasons is important. If you're in it because you think it's glamorous then you're going to have a rude awakening. Making it as a top-flight reporter or presenter takes a lot of commitment and you'll soon fall by the wayside if your heart isn't in the job. What makes things easier is knowing that television is a wonderful profession to work in. That's why so many people want to work in it. If you ever feel like giving up just remember that the rewards at the end are totally worth it. Converting a dream into reality takes hard work, but as you've just read yourself, it's never impossible.